What Is God Able to Do?

The Devotional Meditations of E. May Coggins

Mill Lake Books

Published by Mill Lake Books
Chilliwack, BC, Canada

Printed by Lightning Source, distributed by Ingram

ISBN: 978-1-998787-13-5

Introduction

My mother, E. May Coggins, was a godly woman. It was no accident. My parents got up early, and my father worked hard for long hours, so my mother would prepare a large breakfast for him. When he had gone to work, Mom would sit down at the kitchen table with a second cup of coffee and "prepare her Sunday school lesson." She had about an hour before it was time to wake the three children for school. That in-depth study of the Bible changed her life.

For decades, my mother taught Sunday school in the small Baptist church in our small town of Waterford, Ontario. She began with elementary school children, and in her later years she taught adult Sunday school. I knew she often went to "mission circle" when I and the other children were at school. There were actually several mission circles in the church, gatherings of women who prayed for missions.[1] I knew Mom attended, but what I did not know was that she was a frequent speaker at these meetings and even in regional meetings of mission circles from other Baptist churches. She was humble and not one to publicize her achievements.

---

[1] The mission circle was formed in 1885 and was named the Clara Hellyer Mission Circle in 1963. It met in the afternoon. A second mission circle that met in the evening was formed in 1958. It was named Nancy Mitchell Mission Circle and was later renamed the Mary Wilton Mission Circle. The mission circles prayed and also made bandages and supplies for mission hospitals. There was also a Ladies Aid group (later called Women's Auxiliary), which sewed quilts and other things and which began holding joint meetings with the Clara Hellyer Mission Circle in 1967 (but with separate secretaries and treasurers). Mom was involved in the Clara Hellyer Mission Circle and the Women's Auxiliary, but not the Nancy Mitchell/Mary Wilton Mission Circle, although it appears that she was occasionally a guest speaker there.

Mom was also somewhat of a packrat. After she died, we found among her possessions many of the "meditations" she had prepared for mission circle meetings and other occasions. It is those meditations that have been collected in this volume. They are presented here mostly as they appeared in her notes, with occasionally a few words added to fill in the gaps.

My mother did not just read the Bible. She studied it. According to her notes, she also read many of the key Christian books of her time, some that she owned and many from the church library. These included:

- Hannah Whitall Smith, *The Christian Secret of a Happy Life.*
- John Edmund Haggai, *How to Win over Worry.*
- Raymond J. Davis, *Fire on the Mountains: The Story of a Miracle: The Church in Ethiopia* (Sudan Interior Mission, 1981).
- Andrew Murray, *Waiting on God.*
- Howard G. Hendricks, *Teaching to Change Lives.*
- Grace Noll Crowell, *Riches of the Kingdom: Devotions for Women* (New York" Abingdon Press, 1954).
- Eric Hutchings, *Training for Triumph in Victorious Living* (Zondervan, 1961).
- *The Art of Happiness.*
- Donald M. Mathers, *The Word and the Way* (Angus & Robertson, 1962).
- Bruce Larson, *Dare to Live Now.*
- *Hidden Springs.*
- John Phillips, *I'll Take the High Road* (Emmaus Correspondence Course).
- *Psychology for Living.*
- *None of These Diseases.*
- David J. Pavey, *Quiet, Please! God Sometimes Whispers.*

Mom also read letters and reports from missionaries, and a variety of Christian and other magazines, including:

- *Sunday School Times*
- *The Link & Visitor*

- *The Canadian Baptist*
- *Canadian Bible Society newsletter*
- *Moody Monthly*
- *Power for Living*
- *Mennonite Brethren Herald*
- *Maclean's*

This volume of meditations offers insight into life, particularly Christian and church life, in a previous century. It might perhaps be considered an historical source document, maybe even an historical curiosity or a relic of a bygone era. For sure, my mother had a view of life that would be unusual today. Among the foundational beliefs flowing through these meditations are these insights:

- Life is hard.
- Faith is hard.
- We are here on this earth to serve.
- We can find God in everyday things and activities and in ordinary people.

It is true that these ideas now seem quaint and old-fashioned. But that is their power and importance. The meditations presented here offer a corrective to our own modern biases. They contain wisdom and insights from a previous generation that can help us today, and in that sense they are as relevant today as they were in the last century, perhaps even more relevant.

History often focuses on the thoughts and acts of the great and powerful, while the life of ordinary people is forgotten. My mother was just an ordinary Christian speaking to other ordinary Christians in her small town church. And yet an ordinary Christian, a believer in an extraordinary God, can have a significant impact, perhaps an even greater impact simply because she is ordinary. Jesus' first disciples were all ordinary men who had been with Jesus (Acts 4:13). Gandalf, in J.R.R. Tolkien's masterful trilogy *The Lord of the Rings*, said: "Saruman believes it is only great power that can hold evil in check, but that is not what I have found. I've found it is the small, everyday deeds of ordinary folk that keep the darkness at bay. Simple acts of kindness and love." That is what this volume is all about—the thoughts of an ordinary woman, believing in an extraordinary God, encouraging other ordinary people to believe in the light and to devote themselves to simple acts of kindness and love.

– James R. Coggins

Table of Contents

Why Do We Pray?[2]

Let us spend a little while tonight thinking about the subject of prayer. First of all, let us ask ourselves this question: Why do we pray? I wonder if we don't sometimes make our prayers to God from force of habit. We let it become a mechanical process and do not stop to consider why it is that we pray at all.

I think that perhaps one reason is that we feel our need of God. There are certain times in our lives when we feel that life is too much for us and we are faced with problems. But we find that somehow through prayer our problems disappear.

Then we have the example of Christ, who spent much of His time in prayer. Several times in the Gospels, Jesus spoke to His disciples on the subject of prayer. We read in our Scripture lesson tonight that Christ said, "Your Father knows the things you have need of before you ask Him" (Matthew 6:8). Even though Jesus affirmed that God knows our needs, in the next verse, He said, "In this manner, therefore, pray..." (Matthew 6:9).

Next, we may consider the question: For what should we pray?

In John 14:13-14, we read: "Whatever you ask in My name, that I will do, that the Father may be glorified in the Son. If you ask anything in My name, I will do it." Does this mean that we can ask for anything we want and receive it? Saying Jesus' name at the end of a prayer is not like signing a cheque to make it valid or like some magic formula such as rubbing Aladdin's lamp. No, to pray in Jesus' name means more than that. It means to pray in Jesus' spirit and ask for things which would be in accordance with His teaching and in an attitude that would meet with His approval. If we use this as our standard, will we ever pray for anything that is selfish or unworthy?

---

[2] First devotional, St. Clair Avenue Church Young People's Group, Toronto, 1941. For a time, Mom worked in Government of Ontario offices in Toronto.

Pray, if thou canst, with hope, but ever pray...
But if for any wish thou darst not pray,
Then pray to God to cast that wish away.[3]

In Mark 11:24, Jesus taught, "Whatever things you ask when you pray, believe that you receive them, and you will have them." We must pray in faith and believe that our prayers will be answered. The story is told of a little girl who, instead of saying "Amen" at the end of her prayers, said "RSVP." She expected an answer to her prayers.

Another thing we should remember is our need of constant prayer. Before any of the great events in Christ's life, He spent much time in prayer. If Jesus felt the need of prayer, surely we need to pray too. So often we fail to recognize that need and pay for our neglect with the loss of power. We become like radios with all the tubes burnt out, and when some great concert is on the air, we are "dead"—our lives do not respond and give forth music. Therefore, let us set aside a portion of every day for prayer and communion with God.

The morning is the gate of day,
But ere you enter there
See that you set to guard it well,
The sentinel of prayer.
So shall God's grace your steps attend,
But nothing else pass through
Save what can give the countersign;
The Father's will for you.
When you have reached the end of day
Where night and sleep await,
Set there the sentinel again
To bar the evening's gate.
So shall no fear disturb your rest,
No danger and no care.
For only peace and pardon pass
The watchful guard of prayer.[4]

---

[3] Hartley Coleridge, "Prayer," *Poems by Hartley Coleridge*, 1851.
[4] Annie Johnson Flint, "The Sentinel."

New Year's Devotional[5]
Psalm 90:1-6,12,14, 91:1-4, 92:1-2

For me, Psalm 90 is always associated with New Year's, and I can still remember some of the sermons I have heard that were based on it. One especially that comes to mind was on the text: "Teach us to number our days, that we may gain a heart of wisdom" (Psalm 90:12). At the time, I found it a little frightening, as it seemed to point out just how short life is. But, on the other hand, it points out the eternal, unchanging nature of God. Sometimes we get a little frightened and upset at all the changes going on in the world around us. We think how peaceful life used to be when we were growing up and think we would like to go back—is this why so many people are interested in antiques?—but we are told that this is impossible. It is comforting to know that we have a God who does not change (Malachi 3:6) and who is "from everlasting to everlasting" (Psalm 41:13, 90:2, 103:17, 106:48). It is when we compare our lifespan with God's eternity that it seems we are like grass.

But as I read this Psalm over this week, I felt that Psalm 90 is not complete without the next two Psalms also. In Psalm 91:1-2, we are told: "He who dwells in the secret place of the Most High shall abide under the shadow of the Almighty. I will say of the Lord, 'He is my refuge and my fortress; my God, in Him I will trust.'" Even though God is so great that next to Him we are like grass that grows up and flourishes in the morning but is cut down and withers in the evening (Psalm 90:5-6), and even though, as Isaiah 40:15 says, the nations are as a drop in a bucket—yet there is a secret place where we can find refuge.

One advantage of getting older is that one begins to see a little of the greatness of God and how He has worked things out in our lives.

---

[5] Prepared for January 14, 1976, but postponed; mission study given instead.

One other New Year's sermon that seemed to remain with me had the theme: "I am resolved God's will to know, God's will to do, and God's will to love." We learn God's will through reading our Bibles and through prayer (Psalm 90:12: "Teach us to number our days, that we may gain a heart of wisdom."). To do God's will is a little harder, but when we obey, we find we are dwelling "in the secret place of the Most High God" (Psalm 91:1-2) and we will learn to love God's will: "It is good to give thanks to the Lord, and to sing praises to Your name, O Most High; to declare Your lovingkindness in the morning, and Your faithfulness every night" (Psalm 92:1-2). It is when we learn to love God's will that we are able to show forth His lovingkindness and faithfulness.

Songs of Praise[6]
Psalm 8

In studying the Psalms, one cannot help but notice how many of them are in praise of God:
• "The earth is the Lord's, and all its fullness" (Psalm 24:1).
• "The earth is full of the goodness of the Lord" (Psalm 33:5).
• "O Lord, how manifold are Your works! In wisdom You have made them all. The earth is full of Your possessions" (Psalm 104:24).
• "Oh, that men would give thanks to the Lord for His goodness, and for His wonderful works to the children of men!" (Psalm 107:8).
Were these songs of praise a result of the years David had spent on the hills caring for his sheep? Other great men of the Bible spent years by themselves in the open air. Moses was a shepherd at the time of his call, and we are told that John the Baptist "was in the deserts till the day of his manifestation to

---

[6] Goodwill Bible Class, September 1956. This was the senior adult Sunday school class at Waterford Baptist Church.

Israel" (Luke 1:80). Jesus, too, often felt the need of getting away by Himself for prayer and meditation.

I wonder what David would have written if he had had the opportunities for travel that we have today. Just think of the endless variety of scenery which God has provided for us even in our own province of Ontario—the hills and rocks and forests of northern Ontario, the farmlands of this region, and the St. Lawrence River and Thousand Islands to the east. It seems to me that the more one travels the more one is impressed by the greatness of God. Who but God could have created such beauty?

But perhaps God reveals His true greatness in His care for His people. It is only after we have accepted Christ as our Saviour that we realize the truth of such verses as:

• "Humble yourselves under the mighty hand of God...casting all your care upon Him, for He cares for you" (1 Peter 5:6-7).

• "Your heavenly Father knows that you need all these things" (Matthew 6:32).

• "All things work together for good to those who love God, to those who are the called according to His purpose" (Romans 8:28).

After we have had an experience of the greatness of God in our own lives, we begin to gain some realization of His handiwork in the world about us.

A House of God

In Matthew 7:24-27, Jesus taught us, "Therefore whoever hears these sayings of Mine, and does them, I will liken him to a wise man who built his house on the rock."

Each of us is building a house for God. In any building, it is important to find the right place to build, on a solid rock:

• The apostle Paul described Christians as being part of the "the household of God, having been built on the foundation of the apostles and prophets, Jesus Christ Himself being the chief cornerstone, in whom the whole building, being fitted together, grows into a holy temple in the Lord, in whom you also are being built together for a dwelling place of God in the Spirit" (Ephesians 2:19-22).

• Paul also taught: "For no other foundation can anyone lay than that which is laid, which is Jesus Christ" (1 Corinthians 3:11).

Our house has different rooms:

1. A living room in which to entertain our friends: "Be kindly affectionate to one another with brotherly love...given to hospitality" (Romans 12:10-13).

2. A kitchen and dining room: The Bible provides us with spiritual food. Jesus said, "I am the bread of life" (John 6:35).

3. A library: "Study to shew thyself approved unto God, a workman that needeth not to be ashamed, rightly dividing the word of truth" (2 Timothy 2:15, KJV).

4. A bathroom: "Purge me with hyssop, and I shall be clean; wash me, and I shall be whiter than snow" (Psalm 51:7).

This idea of us being a house for God is repeated several times in the Bible:

• "For we know that if our earthly house, this tent, is destroyed, we have a building from God, a house not made with hands, eternal in the heavens" (1 Corinthians 5:1).

• Jesus promised, "In My Father's house are many mansions; if it were not so, I would have told you. I go to prepare a place for you" (John 14:2).

• "Do you not know that your body is the temple of the Holy Spirit who is in you, whom you have from God, and you are not your own? For you were bought at a price; therefore glorify God in your body and in your spirit, which are God's" (1 Corinthians 6:19-20).

• "You are the temple of the living God" (2 Corinthians 6:16).

• "Do you not know that you are the temple of God and that the Spirit of God dwells in you?" (1 Corinthians 3:16). The apostle then stated that if we are the temple of the living God, we must keep it pure.

The Unfinished Task[7]

Acts 1:1 says that the Gospel of Luke recounted "all that Jesus began both to do and teach." Acts then recounts how Jesus' followers carried on with the task. The hymn says:

He's counting on us the story to tell,
His scheme of redemption for man;
He's counting on you, He's counting on me,
The Master has no other plan.[8]

In the Great Commission, Jesus told His followers to "Go therefore and make disciples of all the nations" (Matthew 28:19). Luke 24:47 says that "Repentance and remission of sins should be preached in His name to all nations, beginning at Jerusalem." On the cross, Jesus said, "It is finished" (John 19:30). He has completed His part of the work, and now it is our turn to take up the task. Jesus said, "If anyone desires to come after Me, let him deny himself, and take up his cross daily, and follow Me" (Luke 9:23). But we can only do this with Jesus empowering us. Jesus said, "Abide in Me, and I in you. As the branch cannot bear fruit of itself, unless it abides in the vine, neither can you, unless you abide in Me. "I am the vine, you are the branches. He who abides in Me, and I in him, bears much fruit; for without Me you can do nothing" (John 15:4-5).

The Unfinished Task 2[9]
Acts 1:1-9

In Acts 1:1, Luke tells us that his "former account"—that is, the Gospel of Luke—described "all that Jesus began both to do and teach." Does this mean that Jesus didn't accomplish all

---

[7] Ladies Aid, April 11, 1956.

[8] C.H. Morris, "His Plan."

[9] Ladies Aid, April 11, 1956; Selkirk Mission Circle, November 8, 1959. Selkirk was another local Baptist church.

He set out to do? Yet, we are told that when Jesus was on the cross, He said, "It is finished!" (John 19:30). He has accomplished His part of the work. Just before His ascension, Jesus gave His followers a task to do for Him. They were to be witnesses for Him throughout the world (Matthew 28:16-20).

What ways are there of witnessing for Him?

First of all, we can tell others about Christ and all He has meant to us. Frank Laubach, who has taught millions of uneducated people to read, has as his motto, "Each one teach one." That is, whenever anyone learns to read, that person should teach someone else. I wonder if that wouldn't be a good motto for Christians. If each person who acknowledges Christ as Saviour would bring someone else to acknowledge Him, would it not make a noticeable difference in our world? And the more we try to pass on to others what we ourselves have learned, the richer our own lives become. If we try to keep on the receiving end of Christianity all the time, our lives become like stagnant pools. The young Christian converts in Bolivia who go out in teams to new areas to preach set us an inspiring example.

Second, we are not only witnesses by telling but also by doing. There is that old saying, "What you are speaks so loudly that I cannot hear what you say." The world often judges us more by our deeds than our words. A candidate for the ministry, in telling why he had chosen it for his life work, said, "My father taught the Christian way of life, and my mother lived it."

It is said that there are three classes of people in the world. There are some who do not even live up to the least that society expects of them. Then there are those who more or less willingly do their duty. But there is another group, and they are the happiest of all. They represent surplus goodness and are always willing to go the second mile. This is one of the costs of discipleship laid down by Jesus.

Perhaps we may feel we would like to assist with God's work but we don't know where to begin or perhaps we haven't the time. Opportunities for service come to us every day. No matter where our lot is cast, there is opportunity to live for Him, there is some task awaiting us, and what might seem at first to be an interruption might be a call to serve God. Consider this poem by Hermann Hagedorn:

There are strange ways of serving God.
You sweep a room or turn a sod,
And suddenly, to your surprise,
You hear the whir of seraphim
And find you're under God's own eyes
And building palaces for Him.

It is said that if God wants someone for a special task, He always goes to someone who is busy. Moses and David were both called when they were looking after their sheep; Elisha was ploughing with twelve yoke of oxen; Gideon was threshing; Peter, Andrew, James, and John were fishing; and Matthew was busy at his tax collector's desk. Yet, they left their work to begin a greater task.

When we read these stories, we also learn that when God called someone to a task, He always provided them with the strength and ability to do it and promised His help. When Moses was called by God, he did not feel that he was able to speak to the people, but God provided Aaron as a spokesman. To Joshua God offered courage: "Be strong and of good courage; do not be afraid, nor be dismayed, for the Lord your God is with you wherever you go" (Joshua 1:9). When Jesus commissioned His followers, He promised, "Lo, I am with you always, even to the end of the age" (Matthew 28:20).

As we read the Bible stories, we sometimes wonder why God chose such humble people to work with Him. Yet we find that when these people were willing to put their small talent in God's hands and work in partnership with Him, they were able to overcome all obstacles. By accepting God's plan for our lives, we can make of them something far greater than we could ever work out for ourselves. Isaiah 40:29-31 promises, "He gives power to the weak, and to those who have no might

He increases strength. Even the youths shall faint and be weary, and the young men shall utterly fall, but those who wait on the Lord shall renew their strength; they shall mount up with wings like eagles, they shall run and not be weary, they shall walk and not faint." By accepting God's help, we may learn to say, "I can do all things through Christ who strengthens me" (Philippian 4:13).

Sometimes today, the difficulty seems to be not in finding something to do but in deciding which of the demands on our time we should accept. Perhaps it would help here if we remembered the parable of the vine and the branches. Christ said in John 15:5: "I am the vine, you are the branches. He who abides in Me, and I in him, bears much fruit; for without Me you can do nothing." Then, after we have learned what it means to abide in Him, we will be ready to follow the command of Jesus: "If anyone desires to come after Me, let him deny himself, and take up his cross daily, and follow Me" (Luke 9:23).

Life is not measured by our years
Or fears or by our worldly tears or cares.
Life is measured and treasured
By our dreams, our hopes, our faith, our love, our deeds,
our prayers.

Today, it seems that whenever we listen to TV or radio advertisements, we are continually being offered a bonus. By buying a certain kind of soap or cereal, we can get an extra gift or premium. The Bible is never out of date, and it offers us the greatest premium of all. We are told that God is "able to do exceedingly abundantly above all that we ask or think" (Ephesians 3:20).

The Heavenly Vision[10]

In 2 Corinthians 11:24-33, we read of the sufferings which Paul endured because he had followed Christ. Why was he willing to do this? Why didn't he give up witnessing for Christ and live like those around him instead of trying to change their lives? He might have said to himself, "There are so few Christians, and they have so many enemies. It is no use trying to evangelize the world." But did he do this? No, as long as he lived, he was a faithful witness for Christ.

Before Paul was taken as a prisoner to Rome, he was taken to King Agrippa, where he was given a chance to tell his story. He told the king of his early life and of the vision of Christ he had on the Damascus road and how Christ had told him he was to be a witness for Him. Then he said, "Therefore, King Agrippa, I was not disobedient to the heavenly vision" (Acts 26:19). This is how Paul explained his career. A heavenly vision had changed his life.

Paul lived many centuries ago. What about our lives today? Have our lives been changed by a heavenly vision? Have these Bible stories become so familiar to us that we cease to marvel at them? If we had a vision such as Paul's, could we help obeying? And yet the call of Christ comes to all of us: "Behold, I stand at the door and knock" (Revelation 3:20).

If we answer the call, what then? If we are a follower of Christ, does He not have a task for us to do just as there was for Paul? After all, there are still millions of people who have never had the opportunity of hearing the gospel story. Just last week, Miss Chitton, a missionary to India, told of one section of India having a population of 300,000 and only 450 of them Christians. Even though we live in a so-called Christian country, there is still a task for us if we look for it. Opportunities for service come to us daily if only we are aware of them.

---

[10] Women's Missionary Society, April 1954.

Albert Schweitzer wrote: "He comes to us as One unknown, without a name, as of old by the lakeside, He came to those men who knew Him not. He speaks to us the same words: 'Follow thou me!' and sets us the tasks which He has to fulfil for our time. He commands. And to those who obey Him, whether they be wise or simple, He will reveal Himself in the toils, the conflicts, the sufferings which they shall pass through in His fellowship, and, as an ineffable mystery, they shall learn in their own experience Who He is."[11]

In order to have true fellowship with Him, we must be obedient to His commands. And if we truly obey Him, there will also be hardships and suffering. Paul said in Philippians 3:10: "That I may know Him, and the power of His resurrection, and the fellowship of His sufferings, being conformed to His death." Christ has not promised His followers an easy life, but He did say, "Lo, I am with you always" (Matthew 28:20).

However, any hardships we endure are not to be compared to those who serve Him on the mission field. Especially is this true in Bolivia, where many have known the fellowship of His suffering. It was only five years ago that Rev. Norman Dabbs, the national pastor Carlos Meneses, and six church members were killed. To be a missionary in Bolivia today is no easy calling. Are we supporting the missionaries as well as we might with our prayers and gifts? Let us, like Paul, not be disobedient to the Heavenly Vision.

Lessons from the Peanut

1. When you look at a peanut, you will notice that it is usually crooked. This is a reminder that there is something wrong with every one of us. We are not perfect.

---

[11] Albert Schweitzer, *The Quest of the Historical Jesus: A Critical Study of its Progress from Reimarus to Wrede.*

2. Peanuts have a double covering—the outer shell and then a dark brown husk on the nut itself. This is a reminder that we cannot see what is inside people. Sometimes people are different at home than they appear in public.

3. Peanuts develop in the dark (underground). We cannot see what is developing inside people.

4. "Consider the work of God; for who can make straight what He has made crooked?" (Ecclesiastes 7:13). Not education or money or power can straighten what is crooked, but God can.

5. When you buy peanuts, you throw away the shell to get at the inside. "Man looks at the outward appearance, but the Lord looks at the heart" (1 Samuel 16:7). Only God knows our hearts.

6. There are two peanuts in every shell. People can work better together.

7. A peanut has no value unless it is broken. Often the same is true of people.

8. All peanuts are the same colour on the outside. "For all have sinned and fall short of the glory of God" (Romans 3:23).

What Is God Able to Do?

• "Without faith it is impossible to please him, for he who comes to God must believe that He is, and that He is a rewarder of those who diligently seek him" (Hebrews 11:6).

• "Now to Him who is able to do exceedingly abundantly above all that we ask or think, according to the power that works in us, to Him be glory in the church by Christ Jesus to all generations, forever and ever" (Ephesians 3:20-21).

What is God able to do?

1. To save us from our sins.

• "He has not dealt with us according to our sins, nor punished us according to our iniquities. For as the heavens are high above the earth, so great is His mercy toward those who fear

Him. As far as the east is from the west, so far has He removed our transgressions from us" (Psalm 103:10-12).
• "You shall call his name Jesus, for He will save His people from their sins" (Matthew 1:21).
• "God was in Christ reconciling the world to Himself, not imputing their trespasses to them" (2 Corinthians 5:19). He has reconciled with us, changing us from enemies to friends.

2. To provide for us.
• Since the Lord is my shepherd, "I shall not want" (Psalm 23:1).
• He gives us rest and peace: "He makes me to lie down in green pastures; He leads me beside the still waters" (Psalm 23:2).
• He gives us guidance: "He leads me in the paths of righteousness for His name's sake" (Psalm 23:3).
• He gives us comfort and help in times of trouble: "Yea, though I walk through the valley of the shadow of death, I will fear no evil; for You are with me; Your rod and your staff they comfort me" (Psalm 23:4).
• "My God shall supply all your need according to His riches in glory by Christ Jesus" (Philippians 4:19).

3. To keep us.
• He gives us protection in times of danger and help when we face temptation: "Behold, I am with you and will keep you wherever you go" (Genesis 28:15).

The Outside Wrapper

1 Samuel 16:7 says, "Man looks at the outward appearance, but the Lord looks at the heart."

At Christmas or on birthdays, we receive gifts. Some are beautifully wrapped. The wrapper protects the gift, but the wrapper is soon discarded. Similarly, people come in various packages. Some have money, cars, and beautiful homes. Others are poorly dressed. One is a fancy package, and the other a poor one.

But inside is the real person.

Sometimes we can see what is inside the wrapper by the way people act.

Seeing beyond First Impressions[12]

At Mission Circle last week, we had an opportunity to see Vera Hayes's art. I had seen some of it years ago and wasn't impressed. It was very plain and only black and white. But when she gave a demonstration of her technique, we saw how the lines were feathered and the empty spaces filled in with tiny designs. This fine detail needs to be seen under a magnifying glass to be appreciated.

Are people like that? Do we just "write them off" instead of hearing their side of the story and finding out that they really are much different from what we had at first thought?

When people hear the name "Mennonite," they think, "Oh, the people who dress in black and use horses instead of cars." But my son is a member of the Mennonite Brethren Church, and that church is not at all like that.

The same night after we saw Vera Hayes's art at Mission Circle, I received a phone call from a man who wanted to come and talk about local history. He lived in a local landmark and was in the process of altering it. His place always looked untidy from the outside, he seemed to keep aloof from the community, and he raised big dogs. But the voice didn't fit the rumours, and we told him to come. We spent a busy three hours digging into local history. When he moved to town, the man had been told, "You will have to live here a lifetime before you will be accepted and become one of us."

---

[12] Goodwill Bible Class, February 13, 1987.

Are we afraid of those who are different? When Ukrainians first came to Bealton,[13] we were told to call them "new Canadians." But more often they were called "foreigners," and there were often battles between them and other children on the way home from school. But, after a generation, the two groups mixed together.

John 1 says that Jesus, who made the world, was in the world, and the world did not know Him. Jesus came in a different way from what He was expected to and was put to death.

Missionaries now going to foreign countries confer with local people and work out a program consistent with their way of life in order to be successful.

The Goodwill Bible Class has been together for forty years. We feel comfortable with each other's company. Is that why newcomers have trouble fitting in?

John 1:10-12 says: "He was in the world, and the world was made through Him, and the world did not know Him. He came to His own, and His own did not receive Him. But as many as received Him, to them He gave the right to become children of God, to those who believe in His name" (John 1:10-12).

The Chariots of God[14]
2 Kings 6:8-17, 2 Corinthians 4:7-10,16-18

In Psalm 104:3, we read that God is the One "who makes the clouds His chariot, who walks on the wings of the wind." Psalm 68:17 says: "The chariots of God are twenty thousand, even thousands of thousands." But chariots are out of date in

---

[13] Bealton, Ontario, is the small community where May Coggins went to school after she came to Canada in 1920 and where she mostly lived until after World War Two.

[14] Clara Hellyer Mission Circle, February 11, 1970.

these modern days, and even when they were in use, they were only for kings and extremely rich people.

It is February 1970, and we are just starting the 1970s. Both religious and secular magazines this winter have been looking back at the 1960s and seeing them as a time of violence, lawlessness, and declining morals. When we look back at the turbulent 1960s, we see mini-skirts and mini-morals. When we look ahead to the 1970s, we see many negative trends—TV, liquor, drugs, Sunday opening of stores, and more. All wonder what is ahead in the next ten years.

A United Church survey showed that its membership could drop to 180,000 (the size of our denomination) ten years from now. The United Church paid $180,000 for a firm of professional planning consultants to survey their Toronto churches. The consultants concluded that these churches might cease to exist in ten years' time. In contrast, the Bible Society newsletter says that Earth's population will increase by one billion people in ten years. Even in our local Baptist church, I heard a member wondering what our church will be like in another ten years. *The Link & Visitor*[15] says that two questions the majority of people ask are "How can I lose weight?" and "Where can I park my car?" The Canadian Bible Society states in its February newsletter that "During the decade we are now entering, the population of the world will increase by one billion."

As we think of the magnitude of our problems, let us read 2 Kings 6:8-17. In this passage, the king of Syria sent a great army to capture the prophet Elisha. When Elisha's servant saw the enemy army surrounding the city, he was dismayed and said, "Alas, my master! What shall we do?" Elisha answered, "Do not fear, for those who are with us are more than those

---

[15] This was a missions publication. When Waterford Baptist Church Mission Circle began in 1885, a few members subscribed to *The Missionary Link*, and in 1891 *The Baptist Visitor* (at $0.10 per year) was introduced. These later joined to become *The Link & Visitor*.

who are with them." Then Elisha prayed that the servant's eyes would be opened, "And behold, the mountain was full of horses and chariots of fire all around Elisha" (2 Kings 6:8-17). The mountain was filled with God's horses and chariots of fire.

Like the servant in our Scripture reading, we wonder if things are hopeless, and we wonder where God is. Perhaps we need a spring tonic. Sometimes, like Elisha's servant, we need to take a second look to see the forces on our side and to be reminded that the things that are seen are temporal but the things that are not seen are eternal. If we leave God out of the picture, our problems look very big and very bad. The January *Moody Monthly* contained an article titled "What's Right with the Church." The author reminded us that history is on our side and just when things seem at their worst, God is still behind the scenes and still in control. In the era of the French Revolution, when the forces of atheism seemed on the rise, God used John Wesley to initiate the evangelical revivals and William Carey to launch the modern missionary movement. A few years ago, *The New Testament in Today's English* (*Good News for Modern Man*) was first published. In 1967 and 1968, it outsold every other paperback. It sold 4,768,000 copies in 1968 alone and is expected to head the list of all-time best sellers by 1990.

A hundred years ago, in 1870, a book was published titled *The Christian's Secret of a Happy Life*. It was written by Hannah Whittal Smith, a Quaker in Philadelphia, and has sold over 200,000 copies. She seemed to be a very practical person. At the beginning of her book, on page 15, she said, "Religion is not something to make us miserable but something to make us happy." Hannah was not frightened by world conditions and what would happen tomorrow. On page 146, she wrote, "Nothing can harm us unless it be God's will." Hannah was not worried that she might not have enough money for the future. She wrote: "It is not necessary for a child to carry a purse" (page 167). At the end of the book, she devoted a whole chapter to the chariots of God and told us that the cares which come to us are really God's chariots. She concluded, "We may be crushed by difficulties or ride over them" (page 229).

In last Sunday's *Power for Living*, there was an article titled "What Women Can Do in These Crisis Days." The head educational consultant for General Motors stated, "Every individual, no matter what remote area of the world he may live in or how insignificant he might be, influences 160 people in his lifetime." Yet Billy Graham states that ninety-five percent of Christians are living a defeated, miserable life.

In 2 Corinthians 4:7-10,16-18, Paul taught: "We have this treasure in earthen vessels, that the excellence of the power may be of God and not of us. We are hard-pressed on every side, yet not crushed; we are perplexed, but not in despair; persecuted, but not forsaken; struck down, but not destroyed—always carrying about in the body the dying of the Lord Jesus, that the life of Jesus also may be manifested in our body...Therefore we do not lose heart. Even though our outward man is perishing, yet the inward man is being renewed day by day. For our light affliction, which is but for a moment, is working for us a far more exceeding and eternal weight of glory, while we do not look at the things which are seen, but at the things which are not seen. For the things which are seen are temporary, but the things which are not seen are eternal."

Let us remember these three verses:
• "Do not fear, for those who are with us are more than those who are with them" (2 Kings 6:16).
• "We have this treasure in earthen vessels, that the excellence of the power may be of God and not of us" (2 Corinthians 4:7).
• "The things which are seen are temporary, but the things which are not seen are eternal" (2 Corinthians 4:18).

Why Is the Bible Like a Valentine?

Tuesday will be Valentine's Day. How do you celebrate Valentine's Day? School children give valentines to their classmates. There are valentine boxes full of candies.

Who was Valentine? He was a Roman Christian who was martyred about 270 AD.

Why do you send valentines? To tell other people how much you love them.

A valentine usually has a message inside. Did you know God has sent a valentine to you? What is it? Can you think of Bible verses telling of God's love?

Why do we have hearts on valentines?

• "Man looks at the outward appearance, but the Lord looks at the heart" (1 Samuel 16:7).

• "The heart is deceitful above all things, and desperately wicked: who can know it?" (Jeremiah 17:9).

• "Trust in the Lord with all your heart, and lean not on your own understanding" (Proverbs 3:5).

Valentine's Day[16]

On Valentine's Day, the theme for our devotional is God's love, as described in God's valentine message to us, the Bible. From ancient times, we are reminded of God's love and concern for us:

• "I have loved you with an everlasting love" (Jeremiah 31:3).

• "As the Father loved Me, I also have loved you; abide in My love. If you keep My commandments, you will abide in My love, just as I have kept My Father's commandments and abide in His love. These things I have spoken to you, that My joy may

---

[16] Afternoon Mission Circle, February 14, 1968.

remain in you, and that your joy may be full. This is My commandment, that you love one another as I have loved you. Greater love has no one than this, than to lay down one's life for his friends. You are My friends if you do whatever I command you" (John 15:9-14).

• "Beloved, let us love one another, for love is of God; and everyone who loves is born of God and knows God. He who does not love does not know God, for God is love. In this the love of God was manifested toward us, that God has sent His only begotten Son into the world, that we might live through Him. In this is love, not that we loved God, but that He loved us and sent His Son to be the propitiation for our sins. Beloved, if God so loved us, we also ought to love one another" (1 John 4:7-11).

• "Behold what manner of love the Father has bestowed on us, that we should be called children of God! Therefore the world does not know us, because it did not know Him. Beloved, now we are children of God; and it has not yet been revealed what we shall be, but we know that when He is revealed, we shall be like Him, for we shall see Him as He is" (1 John 3:1-2).

Christianity is the acceptance of the gift of friendship of Jesus. But how do we start? The Bible is filled with impossible demands.[17] Life is meant to be an adventure, but all of us are being trapped by some hopeless situation that can stifle the joy and adventure and fulfillment. No one is immune. On the other hand, we believe in God's love for us, which is not conditioned by our goodness, and in His power to release and transform us. "Lord, forgive us for running all over the country telling people about Jesus and then being grumpy at home."[18]

Love is God's greatest weapon. How can we learn to love God's way?

---

[17] This idea might be taken from Donald M. Mathers, *The Word and the Way* (Angus & Robertson, 1962), p. 153.

[18] This section might be taken from the book, *Dare to Live Now* by Bruce Larson.

Receiving

1. Christ loves us just as we are. When I become critical of others, I don't need more patience but rather time alone to let God remind me of His love for me: "But God demonstrates His own love toward us, in that while we were still sinners, Christ died for us" (Romans 5:8).

2. We must be ourselves at all times and must not repress the feelings that are wrong. Instead, we must let them come out where God can deal with them.

Transmitting

1. Let others be themselves. We must learn that it is not our job to change other people. Our job is to love them or to let God change us so we can love them. Ponder this quote: "Do you want to be right, or do you want to be well?"[19]

2. Believe in Christ's love for every person we meet. As we approach the time of the coming crusade,[20] we need to remember this. We can always see others who we think should be changed by the crusade, but Jesus reminds us in Matthew 7:3, "Why do you look at the speck in your brother's eye, but do not consider the plank in your own eye?" Perhaps, if in the next ten days we can gain a new idea of God's love for us, then during the crusade we will have the power to pass on that love and concern to others.

Finally, in spite of all our failures, we are reminded in Romans 8:38-39: "Neither death nor life, nor angels nor principalities nor powers, nor things present nor things to come, nor height nor depth, nor any other created thing, shall be able to separate us from the love of God which is in Christ Jesus our Lord."

---

[19] The might be from a book titled *Hidden Springs*.

[20] This was a series of evangelistic meetings held in Waterford Baptist Church. A crusade held about this time had a significant impact on a number of people, including me.

Soap

The money from our special collection this year is going to help build a health post in Bolivia. Sometimes water is scarce, and the health workers there have to help the people get water—by digging a well or capping a spring. Soap is needed as well as water. But quite often the people can't afford to buy it.

We use soap for washing clothes, washing dishes, and washing hands and faces. It helps kill germs. Soap can clean us on the outside, but when we do wrong things, we feel very bad on the inside, and soap can't help with that. But God can make us clean on the inside. Jesus died for our sins.

Soap costs money. Some people can't afford it. But Jesus never turns anyone away because they haven't any money.

On TV, we hear all kinds of soap advertised because the people who make soap want to sell lots of it. God doesn't do advertising like the soap companies, but in the Bible he tells us all about his cure for sin. We can hear about Jesus when we come to Sunday school. He loves us very much and wants to make us clean on the inside.

Pencils

Pencils are like people. They come in all sizes and colours. Yet all have a purpose in life. They all have hearts (it is what is inside that gives them purpose and usefulness). And all write something (leave a mark) on those they meet (come into contact with).

Some pencils are long. Some people have long lives. Some pencils are short. Some people don't live as long.

The usefulness of a pencil depends on the lead inside. Some leads are soft and write easily. Others are hard and tear the paper.

Pencils do not grow in the woods. They were made by an intelligent person. People are made by God.

Pencils represent death. A tree had to be cut down and then cut into small pieces in order to make pencils. Similarly, there can be no Christians without the death of Christ.

A pencil has to be given a new heart. The heart of the wood is removed, and a heart of graphite is inserted. When we become Christians, God gives us a new heart.

Pencils must be sharpened. Similarly, we need to study and prepare ourselves to be useful.

Some pencils are not what they seem. They are a different colour on the inside than they are on the outside. Similarly, some people are hypocrites, different on the inside than they pretend to be.

Some pencils are automatic. The lead must be forced out. Similarly, the Christian often finds God changing his life.

Some pencils are expensive. Some are cheap. Which writes best? It depends on the person holding the pencil. If we place ourselves in God's hand, He can use us.

Pencils have the name of their maker on them. God's servants "shall see His face, and His name shall be on their foreheads" (Revelation 22:4). "He who overcomes, I will make him a pillar in the temple of my God, and he shall go out no more. I will write on him the name of My God, and the name of the city of My God, the new Jerusalem, which comes down out of heaven from My God. And I will write on him My new name" (Revelation 3:12).

Most pencils have an eraser. We make many mistakes. Only Jesus can take away the marks of sin.

Dandelions

Dandelions grow on rich people's lawns and poor people's lawns or along the roadway or in fields. They are the first flower in the spring and the last flower in the fall. The dandelion can teach us some important lessons.

1. A dandelion is always bright and cheerful. It comes up wherever a seed is planted and is just as beautiful away off in a corner of the yard as it is on the front lawn. We are each in a special place God has chosen for us. A dandelion always grows a little taller than the grass around it.

2. A dandelion doesn't get discouraged. We can cut off one flower, but another grows in its place. It blooms early in spring and late in fall and keeps on working, producing flowers and seeds. It does what it is supposed to do. Do we? Do we do the things God wants us to do, or do we decide to do something else?

3. One dandelion produces many seeds, which grow into new plants. If we do as God wishes and tell others about him, our church and Sunday school will grow.

4. Dandelions are always yellow and make people feel happy. So, too, if we wear a big smile, we will make people feel happier.

5. A dandelion grows out of brown earth and produces yellow flowers. The iris has blue flowers, the violet purple flowers, and roses usually red or pink flowers, each according to its own kind. God has made each of us different, to bloom for him in the way that He intended for us.

Jesus Saves Sinners

Jesus said, "I am come that they might have life, and that they might have it more abundantly" (John 10:10).

1. Who are sinners?
• "For all have sinned and fall short of the glory of God" (Romans 3:23).
• "There is none righteous, no, not one" (Romans 3:10).

2. Why are we sinners?

• "Just as through one man sin entered the world, and death through sin, and thus death spread to all men, because all sinned...by one man's disobedience many were made sinners" (Romans 5:12,19).

3. Can we save ourselves?

• "Nor is there salvation in any other, for there is no other name under heaven given among men by which we must be saved" (Acts 4:12).

• "Not by works of righteousness which we have done, but according to His mercy He saved us, through the washing of regeneration and renewing of the Holy Spirit" (Titus 3:5).

• "For by grace you have been saved through faith, and that not of yourselves; it is the gift of God, not of works, lest anyone should boast" (Ephesians 2:8-9).

4. Is there forgiveness with God?

• "In [Jesus] we have redemption through His blood, the forgiveness of sins" (Colossians 1:14).

5. How can we be saved?

• "Believe on the Lord Jesus Christ, and you will be saved, you and your household" (Acts 16:31).

• "For God so loved the world, that He gave His only begotten Son, that whoever believes in Him should not perish but have everlasting life. For God did not send His Son into the world to condemn the world, but that the world through Him might be saved. He who believes in Him is not condemned; but he who does not believe is condemned already, because he has not believed in the name of the only begotten Son of God" (John 3:16-18).

• "If you confess with your mouth the Lord Jesus and believe in your heart that God has raised Him from the dead, you will be saved. For with the heart one believes unto righteousness; and with the mouth confession is made unto salvation" (Romans 10:9-10).

6. Can anyone be saved?

• "Whoever calls on the name of the Lord shall be saved" (Romans 10:13).

• "Look to Me, and be saved, all you ends of the earth!" (Isaiah 45:22).

7. How do we know that we are saved and have eternal life?

• "Most assuredly, I say to you, he who hears my word and believes in Him who sent Me has everlasting life, and shall not come into judgment, but has passed from death into life" (John 5:24).

• "Most assuredly, I say to you he who believes in Me has everlasting life" (John 6:47).

8. Do we sin after we are saved? If we do, can we be forgiven?

• "If we walk in the light as He is in the light, we have fellowship with one another, and the blood of Jesus Christ His Son cleanses us from all sin. If we say that we have no sin, we deceive ourselves, and the truth is not in us. If we confess our sins, He is faithful and just to forgive us our sins and to cleanse us from all unrighteousness" (1 John 1:7-9).

Use Your Gift

In Matthew 25:14-30, Jesus told a parable about a man who gave his servants talents (a weight of money) and then went away, expecting them to put the talents to good use.

In 1 Peter 4:10-11, the apostle Peter applied this message to Christians: "As each one has received a gift, minister it to one another, as good stewards of the manifold grace of God. If anyone speaks, let him speak as the oracles of God. If anyone ministers, let him do it as with the ability which God supplies, that in all things God may be glorified through Jesus Christ, to whom belong the glory and the dominion forever and ever. Amen."

The message is simple. God has given gifts to every Christian. Use your gift!

Prayer

If we can hear astronauts talking from the moon, why should we wonder if our prayers are heard by God?

In John 15:4-11,15-16, Jesus tells us to abide in him and calls us his friends. Prayer is not like pulling a fire alarm, something we do only in an emergency. Prayer is not a pill, to make us better. Prayer is not a last resort, something we do when we have exhausted every other option. Prayer is about having an intimate relationship with God.

Why should we pray?

1. Prayer is commanded by God.

• "Continue earnestly in prayer, being vigilant in it with thanksgiving" (Colossians 4:2).

• "You do not have because you do not ask" (James 4:2).

2. We pray to gain strength and help.

• "As your days, so shall your strength be" (Deuteronomy 33:25).

• "Let us therefore come boldly to the throne of grace, that we may obtain mercy and find grace to help in time of need" (Hebrews 4:16).

3. We pray to find guidance.

• "If any of you lacks wisdom, let him ask of God, who gives to all liberally and without reproach, and it will be given to him" (James 1:5).

4. We pray to have fellowship with God.

• "Abide in Me, and I in you" (John 15:4).

How should we pray?

1. We should pray in Jesus' name.

• "If you ask anything in My name, I will do it" (John 14:14)

2. We should pray according to God's will.

• "Now this is the confidence that we have in Him, that if we ask anything according to His will, He hears us" (1 John 5:14).

3. We should ask for specific things.

What should we pray? The answer is ACTS.

• **A**doration or worship.

• **C**onfession. "Behold, the Lord's hand is not shortened, that it cannot save; nor His ear heavy, that it cannot hear. But your iniquities have separated you from your God; and your sins have hidden His face from you, so that He will not hear" (Isaiah 59:1-2).

• **T**hanksgiving. "In everything give thanks" (1 Thessalonians 5:18).

• **S**upplication and petition. "Be anxious for nothing, but in everything by prayer and supplication, with thanksgiving, let your requests be made known to God" (Philippians 4:6).

Trees

In Genesis 1:11, God said, "Let the earth bring forth grass, the herb that yields seed, and the fruit tree that yields fruit according to its kind." Each tree bears the fruit corresponding to that tree.

In Luke 13:6-9, Jesus told a parable about a man who planted a fig tree and then came to it looking for fruit. He said that if it bore fruit, that would be good, but if it did not, he would have it cut down and thrown away.

In Matthew 7:15-23, Jesus told another parable, saying that just like trees, people bear fruit that reveals their true nature: "You will know them by their fruits....Every good tree bears good fruit, but a bad tree bears bad fruit." He pointed out that some people claim to be followers of God but are "false prophets." Jesus concluded, "Not everyone who says to Me, 'Lord, Lord,' shall enter the kingdom of heaven, but he who does the will of My Father in heaven.'"

Jesus continued that thought in Matthew 25:31-46. There he said that at the end of the world, He would judge people and reward those who had truly served God. How? By feeding the hungry, giving water to the thirsty, taking in strangers, clothing the naked, visiting the sick, and going to those in prison.

Seeds and Roots[21]

After we plant our gardens, we can sit back for a week or two until the seeds come up, but then we have to get to busy with the hoeing and weeding. The weeds in our gardens are easily destroyed when they are small and they do not fight back, but we must continually keep destroying them or they would take over the whole garden. Along the edge of the garden, we have to keep getting rid of the grass roots. And if a garden is not planted for a year or two, it is soon grown over with grass.

If we visit the museum in Toronto, we can see skeletons of huge dinosaurs who once roamed the earth. These were grass-eating animals, and being so huge one would think they would require enormous amounts of grass. Yet suddenly the dinosaurs were destroyed and are now extinct, but the grass is still with us. Why was the grass able to survive when the animals perished? If we think about it, perhaps we would say that it is because the grass has seeds and roots.

Psalm 103:15 says, "As for man, his days are like grass; as a flower of the field, so he flourishes."

In Mark 4, Jesus told the parable of the sower: "Listen! Behold, a sower went out to sow. And it happened, as he sowed, that some seed fell by the wayside; and the birds of the air came and devoured it. Some fell on stony ground, where it did not have much earth; and immediately it sprang up because it had no depth of earth. But when the sun was up it was scorched, and because it had no root it withered away...The sower sows the word. And these are the ones by the wayside where the word is sown. When they hear, Satan comes immediately and takes away the word that was sown in their hearts. These likewise are the ones sown on stony ground who, when they hear the word, immediately receive it with gladness; and they have no root in themselves, and so endure

---

[21] Goodwill Bible Class, May 21, 1980.

only for a time. Afterward, when tribulation or persecution arises for the word's sake, immediately they stumble" (Mark 4:3-6,14-17). In the same parable in Luke 8:11, Jesus explained that "The seed is the word of God." If we plant this seed deep in our hearts, it will help us to survive.

In the parable of the sower, we are told that because some of the plants had no roots, they withered away. But how do we grow good roots? In Colossians 2:7, Paul advises the Colossians to be "rooted and built up in Him and established in the faith, as you have been taught, abounding in it with thanksgiving."

In John 15:5, Jesus spoke of the vine and the branches: "I am the vine, you are the branches. He who abides in Me, and I in him, bears much fruit." If we remain attached to Jesus Christ, we won't need to worry about our roots.

Psalm 1 tells us: "Blessed is the man who walks not in the counsel of the ungodly, nor stands in the path of sinners, nor sits in the seat of the scornful; but his delight is in the law of the Lord, and in His law he meditates day and night. He shall be like a tree planted by the rivers of water, that brings forth its fruit in its season, whose leaf also shall not wither; and whatever he does shall prosper" (verses 1-3).

Jeremiah 17:7-8 repeats this idea: "Blessed is the man who trusts in the Lord, and whose hope is the Lord. For he shall be like a tree planted by the waters, which spreads out its roots by the river, and will not fear when heat comes; but its leaf will be green, and will not be anxious in the year of drought, nor will cease from yielding fruit."

Ephesians 3:17-19 speaks of the Christian "being rooted and grounded in love."

Spring/Joy [22]

Spring seems to be a joyous time of year when all around us we see evidences of new life springing up after the storms of winter. No matter how long the winter, we are reassured by the promise God gave Noah in Genesis 8:22: "While the earth remains, seedtime and harvest, cold and heat, winter and summer, and day and night shall not cease."

There seems to be a certain monotony as we think of the seasons following each other in such an orderly manner, and yet no two springs are exactly alike. We get some idea of the greatness of God as we realize the infinite variety of weather that we get.

At the sod turning [23] on Sunday, I was reminded of how one generation follows another, each living under different conditions, and yet there is a continuity about it as we are reminded that God and His church still remain. Mr. Pursel was born in 1858 and went to Sunday school on this spot before the present church building existed, but there must have been Sunday school teachers passing on God's Word to their scholars. Did they realize that the lessons they taught would almost a century later result in a new building for Christian education?

God's mercy is something like the springtime too. One blessing follows another, and yet there is a great variety in them. Lamentations 3:22-23 tell us: "Through the Lord's mercies we are not consumed, because His compassions fail not. They are new every morning; great is Your faithfulness."

In spite of all the joy and gladness of returning life around us, is this joy always reflected in our lives? A lovely spring day comes along with bright spring sunshine and soft breezes

---

[22] Ladies' Aid, April 13, 1961.

[23] The sod turning, on April 9, 1961, was for the Pursel Building, a Sunday school wing added to Waterford Baptist Church, funded by a bequest from the estate of Llewellyn ("Lewis") Horton Pursel.

blowing, and instead of saying, "This is the day the Lord has made; we will rejoice and be glad in it" (Psalm 118:24), we probably say to ourselves, "What a good day for washing the bedding or airing the drapes." Or is it just that we get a new burst of energy and feel like working once more?

Happiness seems to be a very elusive thing. The more we seek it, the more it eludes us. The *Sunday School Times* this week made the statement that in the Los Angeles area alone, sixty million dollars are spent annually just for the repair of TV sets. This is more than the total annual contributions for foreign missions of the six largest denominations in 1959. I wonder what the figures are for Canada.

Have you noticed how many articles there seem to be lately trying to tell people how to achieve happiness? And they all seem to offer a different solution. I was reading one recently where the writer observed that it had been a long time since he had heard anyone going down the street whistling, and he said that people used to get more fun out of life than they do today. I don't remember much about people whistling, but I do remember how some of the neighbour women used to sing as they went about their housework. Nowadays, instead of hearing singing, we usually hear the TV or radio. It is said that the sense of boredom that so many women feel in connection with housework is because we have so many appliances to make the work easier that we lose the sense of achievement in accomplishing a difficult task.

I wonder, too, if nowadays so much emphasis seems to be placed on getting instead of giving. Everyone seems to be out to get as much as he can for himself. In earlier days, everyone seemed to be more willing to share with their neighbour. When a woman grated the first horseradish, there was always an extra jar or two to be given away. And in the preserving season, the jars of jam and pickles used to pass back and forth.

So often, worldly people seem to get the impression that Christians are very gloomy people and that when people become Christians, they give up everything that is joyful. Is that because we consider Christianity to be a burden (and give people of the world the impression that Christianity is a great burden)? Perhaps instead of trying to carry this great burden around we should see our faith as wings and use it to mount up as eagles (Isaiah 40:31).

Have you ever noticed how many times in the Bible we are told to rejoice?

In reading the Psalms, we cannot help but notice how many are songs of praise: "Bless the Lord, O my soul" or "Give thanks to the Lord" or "Praise the Lord."

Paul, too, was an example of a joyful Christian. Few, if any, have endured more for their faith, yet, as we read the letters he has written, we notice how joyful he appears to be. Do you remember how, in the prison at Philippi at midnight, Paul and Silas prayed and sang praises to God (Acts 16:25)? It would take real joy to sing praises then.

What were the reasons for Paul's joy?

1. Paul said he had learned to be content in whatever state he was in (Philippians 4:11). "Godliness with contentment is great gain" (1 Timothy 6:6).

2. Paul had chosen to forget past mistakes and look forward to the future. "One thing I do, forgetting those things which are behind and reaching forward to those things which are ahead" (Philippians 3:13). Note that Paul said, "One thing I do." Calvin Coolidge said, "We cannot do everything at once, but we can do something at once."

3. Paul put his trust in God. In the first chapter of Philippians, Paul told how the trials that had happened to him had worked out for "the furtherance of the gospel" (Philippians 1:12). Therefore, he was able to say, "For to me, to live is Christ, and to die is gain" (Philippians 1:21). Paul said in Romans 8:28: "We know that all things work together for good to those who love God."

Jesus, too, must have been a joyous person, even though he was a man of sorrows and acquainted with grief (Isaiah 53:3). He seemed to expect us to have peace and joy in our lives if we love Him and believe in Him. Through Him, we have received "beauty for ashes, the oil of joy for mourning, the garment of praise for the spirit of heaviness" (Isaiah 61:3).

At this season, we think of the death and resurrection of Jesus. I recently read an article by D.L. Moody where he asks this question: "Did you know that Christ made a will?" Then, he quoted John 14:27: "Peace I leave with you, My peace I give to you; not as the world gives do I give to you." Jesus rose again to be His own executor and make sure His will was carried out. If Jesus had left His disciples a pot of gold, it would soon have disappeared, but He tells us in John 16:22: "I will see you again and your heart will rejoice, and your joy no one will take from you." Finally, let us remember Jesus' words in John 15:11: "These things I have spoken to you, that My joy may remain in you, and that your joy may be full."

May God grant that each one here today may experience the true joy that comes from God.

Renewal[24]

Spring brings with it the possibility of renewal. Here are some verses that celebrate God's promises of renewal:
• "[The Lord] satisfies your mouth with good things, so that your youth is renewed like the eagle's" (Psalm 103:5).
• "Through the Lord's mercies we are not consumed, because His compassions fail not. They are new every morning; great is Your faithfulness" (Lamentations 3:22-23).
• "Those who wait on the Lord shall renew their strength; they shall mount up with wings like eagles, they shall run and not be weary, they shall walk and not faint" (Isaiah 40:31).
• "Create in me a clean heart, O God, and renew a steadfast spirit within me" (Psalm 51:10).

---

[24] April 4, 1975.

• "Therefore we do not lose heart. Even though our outward man is perishing, yet the inward man is being renewed day by day" (2 Corinthians 4:16).
• "Be renewed in the spirit of your mind" (Ephesians 4:23).

Choices

Moses said to the people of Israel: "See, I have set before you today life and good, death and evil...I have set before you life and death, blessing and cursing; therefore choose" (Deuteronomy 30:15,19). Moses had led the people of Israel through the wilderness for forty years. At the same time, God had led them with a pillar of cloud by day and a pillar of fire by night. God had fed the people with manna and quail and provided water. Now, the people were about to enter the Promised Land, and Joshua had been chosen to be the new leader. At this point, Moses spoke to the people and told them they had to choose between good and evil, life and death.

Some of you may ask: Do we have to choose? The fact is that life is made up of choices. We are continually choosing one thing or another.

Ships on the St. Lawrence River take on a pilot. Why? To guide them along the river. Similarly, we are all on the voyage of life. Each one of us is the captain of our own ship. And we have a destination, either heaven or destruction. We need a pilot (Jesus) to guide us. We have three choices in life. 1. We can steer for the rocks. 2. We can just drift along. 3. Or we can choose Jesus to be our pilot and stay on course. In Deuteronomy 31:8, Moses told Joshua and the people of Israel: "The Lord, He is the One who goes before you. He will be with you, He will not leave you nor forsake you; do not fear nor be dismayed." By making this one big choice, we can get rid of the smaller ones. They will already have been made.

Here are some other verses about making the big choice:

• "Choose for yourselves this day whom you will serve...But as for me and my house, we will serve the Lord" (Joshua 24:15).

• "There is a way that seems right to a man, but its end is the way of death" (Proverbs 14:12).

• "The Lord knows the way of the righteous, but the way of the ungodly shall perish" (Psalm 1:6).

• "Jesus said...'I am the way, the truth, and the life. No one comes to the Father except through Me'" (John 14:6).

• "In all your ways acknowledge Him, and He shall direct your paths" (Proverbs 3:6).

• "Enter by the narrow gate; for wide is the gate and broad is the way that leads to destruction, and there are many who go in by it. Because narrow is the gate and difficult is the way which leads to life, and there are few who find it" (Matthew 7:13-14).

• Jesus said, "I am the door. If anyone enters by Me, he will be saved, and will go in and out and find pasture" (John 10:9).

• "We know that all things work together for good to those who love God, to those who are the called according to His purpose" (Romans 8:28).

• "These words are faithful and true" (Revelation 22:6).

Everyday Saints

1 Corinthians is a letter from the apostle Paul to Christians in the city of Corinth. It starts: "Paul, called to be an apostle of Jesus Christ through the will of God, and Sosthenes our brother, to the church of God which is at Corinth, to those who are sanctified in Christ Jesus, called to be saints, with all who in every place call on the name of Jesus Christ our Lord, both theirs and ours."

Paul said that he was "called to be an apostle."

Paul then said that the members of the church in Corinth were "called to be saints."

Then, notice that it is not only the members of the church at Corinth who are called to be saints but also "all who in every place call on the name of Jesus Christ our Lord."

Wouldn't you say that means that all of us who acknowledge Christ as Saviour and Lord are called to be saints? But we might say that we are just ordinary, everyday people and it would be impossible for us to be saints.

What is a saint? There are many definitions we might give. Our dictionary at home devotes almost a whole page to explaining it, but, after reading it over, I hadn't a clearer idea than before.

On Sunday, I happened to tune into a radio program, which gave the best definition I have heard so far:

A little girl in a large city had been asking what a saint was. One Sunday, when they were near a church, she was attracted by a large stained glass window and asked her mother what it was. Her mother said, "That is a saint," and the little girl said, "Then a saint is a stained glass window." A few days later, they were walking in the park near their home, and they saw an old lady crossing the park. She carried a basket and was on her way to the poorer section of the city. As the mother saw the old lady, she said, "There goes a saint if there ever was one." The little girl was puzzled. She couldn't see what connection there was between the old lady and the stained glass window. She thought for a while and then exclaimed, "Oh, I know now. A saint is a person who lets the light shine through."

If that is the definition, don't you think that perhaps it might be possible for us to be saints? After all, Jesus has said, "Be perfect, just as your Father in heaven is perfect" (Matthew 5:48).

During the war, in countries where there was danger of enemy bombing, the people used heavy blackout material to darken their windows at night. Perhaps we, too, use blackout material (sin, selfishness, greed) so that Christ, the Light of the World, is unable to shine through us. We could perhaps achieve sainthood by removing the blackout material so that others are able to see the Light.

What qualities do we need if we are to be saints?

1. Patience. Revelation 13:10 speaks of "the patience and the faith of the saints." Every individual, no matter what his work, has the opportunity of displaying the patience of a saint—and thus becoming one.

2. Endurance. The Bible talks of the endurance of the saints. Have we enough stability to endure hardship and thus gain endurance?

3. Humility. It has been said, "A real saint doesn't even know he is one." He sees the perfection of Christ so clearly that to himself he seems a sinner.

4. Forgiveness. Christ has told us to forgive "seventy times seven" (Matthew 18:22), and even on the cross He prayed for those who were crucifying Him, "Father, forgive them" (Luke 23:34).

5. Courage. Everyday saints must have courage. Paul spoke of the saints who were "of Caesar's household" (Philippians 4:22). Surely any Christians there would have need of courage and would need to be ready to face persecution.

We may find it difficult to achieve these qualities, but we read in Mark 9:23 that Jesus said, "All things are possible to him who believes."

Even as a stained glass window becomes an inspiration to those who look at it, so, too, our lives can inspire those about us. We may just be ordinary people, but, with God's help, we are all given the opportunity of achieving the status of sainthood.

Good Friday[25]
Ephesians 3:14-21

As Good Friday approaches, we think once more of God's great love for the world and for each of us in particular, in sending His Son to die for us. In this passage, Paul prayed that his readers might be able to comprehend the height, the depth, the breadth, and the length of God's love. With our limited human experience, it is difficult for us to get any idea of the greatness of this love. A boy[26] told me recently that he did not want to live forever because the thought of eternity seemed so great, so beyond his ability to understand, that it terrified him.

We read that "God so loved the world that He gave His only begotten Son, that whoever believes in Him should not perish but have everlasting life" (John 3:16). Annie Johnson Flint has tried to express something of God's love in her poem:

How broad is His love?
Oh, as broad as man's trespass,
As wide as the need of the world can be;
And yet to the need of one soul it can narrow—
He came to the world and He came to me.

How long is His love?
Without end or beginning,
Eternal as God and His life it must be,
For, to everlasting as from everlasting
He loveth the world and He loveth me.

How deep is His love?
Oh, as deep as man's sinning.
As low as the uttermost vileness can be;
In the fathomless gulf of the Father's forsaking

---

[25] Senior Mission Circle, March 22, 1961.
[26] I remember having this conversation with her. It is common for preachers to include illustrations from their own families.

He died for the world and He died for me.

How high is His love?
It is high as the heavens,
As high as the throne of His glory must be;
And yet from that height He hath stooped to redeem us–
He so loved the world and He so loved me.

How great is His love?
Oh, it passeth all knowledge,
No man's comprehension its measure can be;
It filleth the world, yet each heart may contain it–
He so loves the world and He so loves me.[27]

In reading the Easter story, I have been impressed by the fact that the followers of Jesus had to meet Jesus personally before they were really convinced that He was alive. Peter and John ran to the empty tomb but were not convinced until He appeared to them and the other disciples in the upper room. Thomas, who was not in the upper room that first time, did not believe until Jesus appeared again. The two followers of Jesus on the road to Emmaus did not understand until Jesus appeared and began walking with them and explaining things. Paul did not believe until Jesus confronted him on the Damascus road. Do we have a personal experience of Christ? Or is He just a good man who lived and died two thousand years ago?

Before His ascension, Jesus told His disciples: "You shall receive power when the Holy Spirit has come upon you; and you shall be witnesses to Me" (Acts 1:8). A witness in court is not allowed to give hearsay evidence but only something he has seen for himself and knows for a fact.

In our Mission Circle, we heard stories of the witnessing done by new converts in Bolivia. I wonder if because we have

---

[27] Annie Johnson Flint (1866-1932), "The Love of Christ."

always had a church here, we just take it for granted. We perhaps see something that should be done and say the church should do something about that—when perhaps it is a call to us to do something about that. There are certain jobs that each of us can do better than anyone else. Reverend W.G. Coltman said, "The Great Commission, 'Go ye into all the world,' does not apply exclusively to foreign missions, for the world begins where your front yard ends. When you leave your own doorstep, you are in the world."

In closing, I would also like to stress verse 20 of Ephesians 3: "Now to Him who is able to do exceedingly abundantly above all that we ask or think." Those of us in mission circles and churches need to realize the truth of this. If we could just see the results of our prayers, we would probably be more zealous in them. Electricity is a marvel. We can press a button in the house, and a light goes on in the barn.[28] We understand and accept this. But, if I should happen to pray for a missionary in Bolivia or India, I may not know how much that prayer has accomplished. I am too far away to see it. But God's great power and love can easily reach that far, and beyond.

Jesus Lays Down His Life and Takes It Up Again

Mark 15-16 describe the crucifixion of Jesus.

Mark 15 starts by saying that Jesus was brought before Pilate "immediately" (the King James Version says "straightway"). This was after a night trial by the Jews, which was informal and illegal. The Jews had no power to put anyone to death; in the Roman Empire, only a Roman ruler could approve a death sentence (John 19:7-8). So, the Jewish leaders

---

[28] Our family had a large barn some distance from the house, and in the fall of 1955, five years before this mediation, a long trench was dug from the house to the barn for a cable that would bring electricity to the barn.

took Jesus to the Roman governor. Pilate normally lived at Caesarea on the Mediterranean coast but was in Jerusalem for the Passover holiday. Roman officials began their working day at first light, and the Sanhedrin wanted Jesus to be executed as soon as possible. Blasphemy was a religious crime, not a civil offense, but the Jews made it sound as though Jesus was opposing Caesar.

When Pilate asked Jesus if He was the king of the Jews, Jesus answered, "It is as you say." This suggests that Jesus was admitting He wanted to replace Caesar, but Jesus left it up to Pilate to say for sure (and Pilate later gave Jesus the title). After that, Jesus remained silent, which was very unusual for a prisoner on trial. According to John's Gospel, Jesus also said that His kingdom was "not of this world" (John 18:36), and when the Jews said that Jesus claimed to be the Son of God, Pilate became afraid (John 19:7-11). (Note that in Mark 15:39, a centurion confirmed that Jesus was the Son of God.) This all placed Pilate in a difficult position (Mark 15:10). He knew Jesus was innocent but felt the pressure of the crowd and the temple guards. The punishment for blasphemy was stoning to death. Crucifixion was used only on slaves, provincials, and the lowest criminals. Pilate sent Jesus to be crucified "after he had scourged him" (had him whipped).

Consider all that Jesus had gone through. He had been teaching in the temple the day before, followed by the very emotional Last Supper. He prayed in the Garden of Gethsemane in such agony that He sweat drops of blood (Luke 22:44). He was then tried before Annas and Caiaphas, the high priest. Then he was tried by both Pilate and Herod. Jesus must have been worn out from lack of sleep. Herod's men mistreated Him, mocked Him by putting on Him a gorgeous robe, and then sent Him back to Pilate. He then had to carry the cross to the place of execution. On the cross, He refused wine mixed with myrrh (myrrh had been a gift from the wise men at His birth). After the ninth hour, Jesus "cried out with a loud voice" and died (Mark 16:37). People who were crucified usually lasted longer.

Scholars believe that Mark 16:8 is the last verse of Mark's Gospel that has survived. Early copies have two additional endings that were added later.

Easter[29]

Why should an event that took place almost 2,000 years ago affect our lives today?

Most people acknowledge that Jesus did live in Israel, but many are not ready to admit that He was the Son of God. Last week, I read this statement: "For some people, Jesus is still imprisoned in history. They are quite sure that he *was*, but they do not realize that he *is*." But Jesus said in Revelation 1:18, "I am He who lives, and was dead, and behold, I am alive forevermore."

This Easter, I have been reading the story of the resurrection to see if I could find anything I had overlooked before. Matthew 28 says that the guards at Jesus' tomb "shook for fear" and that the women "went out quickly from the tomb with fear and great joy" (verses 4,8). Mark 16:5 says that the women "were alarmed." Luke 24:4-5 says that the women were "greatly perplexed" and "afraid." But then, after the various people became convinced that Jesus really was alive, we read that they ran to pass on the word to their friends. Even when Jesus was parted from them and carried up to heaven, they returned to Jerusalem "with great joy" (Luke 24:52). We may be afraid and perplexed, but if we are absolutely convinced that Jesus is alive, we realize that He is able to turn the fear into joy.

Second, in reading the Easter story, did you notice that each person had to find out for himself before he really

---

[29] Goodwill Bible Class, April 15, 1981.

believed Jesus was alive? The angel invited the women into the tomb to see the place where Jesus had lain. Peter and John didn't believe the women until they had gone and found out for themselves. Thomas, too, asked for definite proof. Jesus seemed to have a special way of convincing each individual. He met Mary Magdalene and called her by name. He ate in front of the disciples and told them to touch and see Him. Peter and John were convinced by the position of the funeral clothes in the tomb. The two at Emmaus recognized Him when He broke bread. Seven disciples recognized Him when He performed a miracle, filling their empty nets with a multitude of fish at the Sea of Galilee (John 21).

There are many books today which describe spectacular experiences. But we should not be envious and should remind ourselves of Jesus' words, "Blessed are those who have not seen and yet have believed" (John 20:29). John Wesley made this statement after he had been converted: "I felt that I did trust in Christ alone for salvation and an assurance was given me that he had taken away *my* sins, even *mine*, and had saved *me* from the law of sin and death." Or we can be like the Samaritans in John 4:42, who said, "Now we believe, not because of what you said, for we ourselves have heard Him and we know that this is indeed the Christ, the Savior of the world."

Third, in Matthew 28:6, the angel told the women to "Come, see the place where the Lord lay," and then in the next verse they were told to "go quickly and tell His disciples." Once we have really become convinced that Jesus is alive, then we are able to go and tell others.

We are given this promise in Jeremiah 33:3: "Call to Me, and I will answer you, and show you great and mighty things, which you do not know." This promise was also given in Jeremiah 29:13: "And you will seek Me and find Me, when you search for Me with all your heart." But we must remember that Easter followed Good Friday and it is often after passing through troubled times that we realize that Jesus is alive and able to help us: "For we walk by faith, not by sight" (2

Corinthians 5:7). "Jesus Christ, whom having not seen you love" (1 Peter 1:7-8).

The Walk to Emmaus[30]
Luke 24:13-35

For many of us, the story of the walk to Emmaus is our favourite story of the resurrection.

When reading Bible stories, we perhaps may dream of the joy that would have been ours if we had been able to see Jesus when He was here in the flesh. We think what a privilege it would have been to have heard His voice or to have watched Him perform His miracles. Or how wonderful it would have been to have witnessed some of the appearances of Christ after His resurrection. But perhaps even more miraculous is the fact that Jesus is the same, yesterday, today, and forever (Hebrews 13:8) and that nearly 2,000 years afterward we may have fellowship with Him and experience in our own lives the reality of His resurrection. We must not allow these dreams to substitute for the deeper spiritual companionship we may have with Jesus now. He Himself extended the invitation when He said, "Abide in Me, and I in you" (John15:4).

How may we have this fellowship with Jesus? Let us consider again the appearances of Christ after His resurrection. Did you ever stop to wonder why Jesus did not reveal Himself in the temple or in the marketplace, where He would have been seen by hundreds of people? Instead, He usually came in quiet and unexpected places to a small group of His followers:
- to these two on the road to Emmaus;
- to the disciples in the upper room;
- to a small group of the disciples who had gone fishing.

---

[30] Mission Circle, March 30, 1960. Also delivered, in a somewhat different form, at one other time.

I wonder if that is why we have trouble having fellowship with Christ today. In the noise and confusion of modern day living, it is difficult to get away to a quiet place where He may make contact with us. In other places in the Bible, we read of people finding God in unexpected places. Moses found Him in a burning bush, Jacob discovered that He was at Bethel, and Paul met Christ on the Damascus road. So today the revelation of God's presence comes to people when they are busy at their daily tasks, struggling with some problem or even travelling the wrong road. One writer has said:

There are strange ways of serving God;
You sweep a room or turn a sod,
And suddenly, to your surprise,
You hear the whirr of seraphim,
And find you're under God's own eyes
And building palaces for him.[31]

Quite often in the stories of the resurrection, we find that when Jesus appeared to His followers, they were speaking or thinking of Him. In the story of the walk to Emmaus, we find that the two followers were talking together about Jesus when He appeared to them. Later, after He had gone away, they returned to Jerusalem to tell the disciples about meeting Jesus. The Bible tells us: "So it was, while they conversed and reasoned, that Jesus Himself drew near and went with them" (Luke 24:15). Jesus said in Matthew 18:20: "Where two or three are gathered together in My name, I am there in the midst of them." Have you ever noticed how much easier it is to speak of Christ when we are with some people and how, leaving them, we feel as though His presence has been very near? If we do not give Him a chance, He is unable to make His presence known to us. Luke 24:29 tells us that the two who met Jesus on the road to Emmaus invited Jesus to stay with them. If we invite Him into our homes, we, too, will receive a

---

[31] Hermann Hagedorn, 1882-1964.

blessing. Such an invitation is implicit where people post the motto: "Christ is the Head of this house."

Have you noticed what a change took place in Christ's followers after they had met their risen Lord? After the crucifixion, they were discouraged and fearful, but when they realized that He was really alive, their lives became filled with joy, and they wanted to tell the good news to others.

Once we have met the risen Christ and realized that He is just as real today as He was then, our lives become changed, and we can never go back to the old way of living. Leslie Weatherhead said, "The reality of Christ's friendship is reached not through argument but through experience. 'The love of Jesus, what it is, none but His loved ones know'—but they know." Each one must experience this himself, and no one can believe for another. The deepest experiences of our lives are often those which we find very difficult to pass on to others. "But as many as received Him, to them He gave the right to become children of God, to those who believe in His name" (John 1:12).

In these days of radio and electricity, it should be so much easier for us to believe it possible to have fellowship with Christ and to feel His presence with us. In order to have light, we merely press a button, and our homes are lit by power generated many miles away. But there are certain conditions which must be fulfilled beforehand. Our homes must be wired for electricity, and the lines connecting us to the source of power must be in good condition. If God's power is to show in our lives, we must make contact with Him through prayer and keep up our lines of communication with Him. So it is with radio. We can listen in on any program we wish as long as we tune in on the proper wavelength. If we wish to know God's will, we must keep our lives tuned in on the right station. There is a story of a minister who complained to a soap manufacturer that the soap was not getting anything clean. After investigation, the manufacturer explained that the problem was that the soap had to be taken out of the box and applied.[32] God has given us many promises, but they won't help us unless we apply them to our lives. Perhaps one of the greatest is: "Lo, I am with you always, even to the end of the age" (Matthew 28:20).

Is God Alive?[33]

2 Timothy 1:6-10, Philippians 3:7-11

Is God dead? Is God alive? Where is the evidence? We believe in the resurrection. We also believe that Jesus said, "Do not worry about tomorrow" (Matthew 6:34) and "Do not lay up for yourselves treasures on earth...but lay up for yourselves treasures in heaven" (Matthew 6:19-20) and "Whoever compels you to go one mile, go with him two" (Matthew 5:41). We say we believe, but when it comes to acting on what we believe, that is different.

The disciples had difficulty believing the resurrection until each one received some personal evidence. Peter had one experience, and Thomas had another. So, today each of us needs to take the trouble to find out for ourselves. This calls for strong faith and great courage, but then life will become an adventure. There has been a great deal of research done. Why can't each of us try to do a little research on our own?

A recent Sunday school lesson talked about "the cost of discipleship." There is a book in our library called *I'll Take the High Road.* There are higher and lower spiritual planes. How do we reach the higher plane?

Consider Jesus' feeding of the multitudes. In Matthew 14, Jesus used five loaves and two fishes to feed 5,000 people, and there were twelve baskets left over. In Matthew 15, Jesus used

---

[32] In many cases, Mom had memorized stories such as this, and her notes say only: "Story of soap manufacturer and minister."

[33] Goodwill Bible Class, January 1972.

seven loaves and a few fish to feed 4,000 people, and there were seven baskets left over. When the boy with the loaves and fishes gave all he had, the miracle was performed. It is a spiritual principle that the greater the need and the fewer the resources, the more that will be left over. Augustine said, "Faith is believing something we cannot see with the result that we see what we believe." How can we reach the higher plane? First, we need faith. The January issue of the *Canadian Baptist* talked about belief and faith—belief is what I base my life on.

Peter Marshall (in "Praying is Dangerous Business") spoke of different kinds of power—fire, explosives, gasoline, electricity, and atomic bombs—but none of these can change human nature. Then he described "a power so great it made atonement for the sins of the world, the ability to live victoriously like children of God in fellowship with Him who made the world and the sun and the moon and the stars. It was a power that would enable believers to do the mighty works of Christ and to experience flowing in and through their own lives the energy of God. This power is obtained by reaching out to God in prayer. The power of prayer is an unexplored field for average believers. When we are willing to accept God's decision in the matter about which we are praying, our prayers will be answered."

Jesus' Last Will and Testament (Whit Sunday)[34]
John 14:1-29

On May 17, some churches celebrate Whit Sunday, when we remember Pentecost and the coming of the Holy Spirit to those gathered in the upper room. In the verses we have read

---

[34] Senior Mission Circle, May 1974.

(John 14:1-29), Jesus was promising the disciples that, after He had left them, He would send them another Helper or Comforter or Counsellor, and at Pentecost the promise was fulfilled. I wonder if perhaps this chapter might be called Jesus' last will and testament. Let us notice some of the things He left His disciples:

1. Real Estate. Jesus said, "I am going to the Father" (John 14:12,28) and "In My Father's house are many mansions; if it were not so, I would have told you. I go to prepare a place for you. And if I go and prepare a place for you, I will come again and receive you to Myself; that where I am, there you may be also" (John 14:2-3).

2. A Cheque (a promise of fruitfulness). Jesus said, "Most assuredly, I say to you, he who believes in Me, the works that I do he will do also; and greater works than these he will do, because I go to My Father" (John 14:12).

3. Another Cheque (answered prayer). Jesus said, "Whatever you ask in My name, that I will do, that the Father may be glorified in the Son. If you ask anything in My name, I will do it" (John14:13-14).

4. A Counsellor. Jesus said, "I will pray the Father, and He will give you another Helper, that He may abide with you forever" and "The Helper, the Holy Spirit, whom the Father will send in My name, He will teach you all things, and bring to your remembrance all things that I said to you" (John 14:16,26).

5. Peace. Jesus said, "Peace I leave with you, My peace I give to you" (John 14:27).

Were these promises just for the disciples? No. John 1:12 says, "As many as received Him, to them He gave the right to become children of God, to those who believe in His name." All of us have our times of doubts and fears, time when we seem far from God. Let us remember that the disciples had their great experiences and times of doubt too. I am sure that all of the disciples must have felt, like Peter, that they would never deny Jesus, and yet they all forsook him. Even in the Garden of Gethsemane, they could not stay awake to watch with him. I am glad we are told of these human frailties because we, too, are weak. It is wonderful to know that we have a God who, in spite of our failures, will never leave or forsake us and is always ready to forgive us.

The disciples had their glorious experiences in the upper room and again at the Ascension and at Pentecost. But between the first two were hours of doubt and despair, and before Pentecost there were long hours of prayer. But after God's Spirit came upon them, they were changed men.

Servants of the Most High God[35]

Babylonian King Nebuchadnezzar called to Shadrach, Meshach, and Abed-Nego in the fiery furnace, "Servants of the Most High God, come out, and come here" (Daniel 3:26). And so they did.

At Philippi, a young slave girl possessed with a spirit of divination followed Paul and his fellow workers, saying, "These men are the servants of the Most High God, who proclaim to us the way of salvation" (Ats 16:17).

When Daniel was in the lions' den, King Darius came to the den early in the morning, and called, "Daniel, servant of the living God, has your God, whom you serve continually, been able to deliver you from the lions?" (Daniel 6:20).

Each of these men must have been outstanding because in each case heathen people recognized that they served a God who was all-powerful.

Today, we as Christians have the opportunity of becoming servants of the living God. Do we realize what possibilities are

---

[35] Villa Nova Mission Circle, May 1981. Villa Nova was another local Baptist church.

open to us and what resources are available to us if we accept the challenge?

The word "servant" is not a popular term today. Everyone wants to be free to do as they please and to run their own lives. But yet in our own families we know that it is not drudgery to serve those we love and do things for them. And, after all, to be a servant of the Most High God, the King of kings, should give the job status.

Before taking a job nowadays, we usually check it out to find our duties and obligations and also the benefits. Perhaps we should also check out what is involved in being servants of the Most High God.

1. The job demands loyalty.

As servants, we must put Christ first in our lives: In Ephesians 6:6, Paul said, "As bondservants of Christ," we should be "doing the will of God from the heart."

2. The job demands time.

It is a full-time job because whatever we are doing—shopping, working, or anything else—we are witnessing as to what kind of people we are:

You are writing a gospel,
A chapter a day
By the deeds that you do,
And the words that you say.[36]

What is the gospel according to you, according to what you do and say?

The job also requires time for Bible study and prayer and time to listen for God's voice. Mrs. Wilton[37] spoke on prayer at our mission circle last week and stressed the need of having a quiet time early in the day. If we keep putting it off until we get everything done, we never get around to it.

---

[36] Poem by Paul B. Gilbert.

[37] Mary Wilton and her husband Lyle joined Africa Inland Mission in 1971 and served in Africa for 35 years in medical and other ministries.

There must also be time allowed for interruptions—people phoning us or coming to us for help. Interruptions are "God rearranging our schedule to suit His plans."

3. The job demands obedience.

In Philippians 2:5, we are told, "Let this mind be in you which was also in Christ Jesus, who...made Himself of no reputation, taking the form of a bondservant...He humbled Himself and became obedient to the point of death."

1 Peter 1:14 tells us that we are to be like "obedient children."

In 1 Samuel 15:22, Saul was told that "to obey is better than sacrifice."

In Jeremiah 7:23, God said, "Obey My voice, and I will be your God."

Our director, Mary Hansen, said last fall that she has had some interesting results when she tells God that she is available if he has some job He wants her to do. Did you ever try praying, "God, what would You like me to do for You today?" It usually brings a quick answer via the phone or doorbell.

4. Sometimes the job of being a servant of the Most High God demands life itself.

In Luke 9:23-24, Jesus said, "If anyone desires to come after Me, let him deny himself, and take up his cross daily, and follow Me. For whoever desires to save his life will lose it, but whoever loses his life for My sake will save it."

Finally, what about the salary?

God promises that if we serve Him, we will have all of our wants and needs supplied, strength for today and hope for tomorrow. He will give us "all these things"—food, clothes, etc. (Matthew 6:33). Philippians 4:19 promises that "God shall supply all your need according to His riches in glory by Christ Jesus."

Revelation 22:14 says: "Blessed are those who do His commandments, that they may have the right to the tree of life, and may enter through the gates into the city."

Obedience[38]

Have you ever noticed how often the topic of obedience comes up in the Bible? Here are just a few of the verses mentioning this important topic:

• "As by one man's disobedience many were made sinners, so also by one Man's obedience many will be made righteous" (Romans 5:19).

• "Let this mind be in you which was also in Christ Jesus, who...humbled Himself and became obedient to the point of death, even the death of the cross" (Philippians 2:5-11).

• "Blessed are those who do His commandments, that they may have the right to the tree of life, and may enter through the gates into the city" (Revelation 22:14).

• "Be sober, and rest your hope fully upon the grace that is to be brought to you at the revelation of Jesus Christ; as obedient children" (1 Peter 1:13-14).

• "Has the Lord as great delight in burnt offerings and sacrifices, as in obeying the voice of the Lord? Behold, to obey is better than sacrifice, and to heed than the fat of rams" (1 Samuel 15:22).

• "Obey My voice, and I will be your God, and you shall be My people. And walk in all the ways that I have commanded you, that it may be well with you" (Jeremiah 7:23).

• "Bondservants, be obedient to those who are your masters according to the flesh, with fear and trembling, in sincerity of heart, as to Christ; not with eyeservice, as men-pleasers, but as bondservants of Christ, doing the will of God from the heart" (Ephesians 6:5-6).

• "Do you not know that to whom you present yourselves slaves to obey, you are that one's slaves whom you obey,

---

[38] There is no evidence that this meditation was ever delivered to any group, but it is typical of many biblical subjects that Mom researched and recorded in a notebook.

whether of sin leading to death, or of obedience leading to righteousness?" (Romans 6:16).

When God Is Invisible[39]
Isaiah 45

Isaiah 45 is a long poem or song. It is addressed to King Cyrus, the founder of the Persian Empire. But the speaker is God. In any Bible study, the logical place to begin is with God.

When studying Sunday school lessons, we are sometimes told that when a Bible verse is repeated, it is something that God wishes us to remember especially. The verse "I am the Lord, and there is no other" is repeated seven times in this chapter (verses 5,6,14,18,21,22).

But, in verse 15, we are told: "Truly You are God, who hide Yourself." We all have days when God seems far away.

Oh, it is hard to work for God,
To rise and take his part
Upon this battlefield of earth
And not sometimes lose heart.
He hides himself so wondrously
As though there were no God.
He is least seen when all the powers
Of ill are most abroad.
Or he deserts us at the hour
The fight is all but lost
And seems to leave us to ourselves
Just when we need him most.

But later in the poem we are told that God is other than we think:

Thrice blest is he to whom is given
The instinct that can tell
That God is on the field

---

[39] Goodwill Bible Class.

When he is most invisible.[40]

Perhaps that is what is meant in verse 3 of Isaiah 45: "I will give you the treasures of darkness and hidden riches of secret places." We may feel that we know God, but it is only when we experience dark days and troubled times that we realize God's presence and know that, no matter what happens, His promises are sure and can be depended on. As for the "hidden riches" and "secret places," perhaps that refers to the need for private devotions and the need to take time to be alone with God. Jesus reminds us in Matthew 6:6: "But you, when you pray, go into your room, and when you have shut your door, pray to your Father who is in the secret place; and your Father who sees in secret will reward you openly." Another promise is in Isaiah 61:3, that God will "give them beauty for ashes, the oil of joy for mourning, the garment of praise for the spirit of heaviness." In Jeremiah 33:3, God promises, "Call to Me, and I will answer you, and show you great and mighty things, which you do not know."

But Luke 12:48 warns us, "For everyone to whom much is given, from him much will be required." I wondered: Just what does God require of me? I looked in the concordance. I found:

• "And now, Israel, what does the Lord your God require of you, but to fear the Lord your God, to walk in all His ways and to love Him, to serve the Lord your God with all your heart and with all your soul, and to keep the commandments of the Lord and His statutes which I command you today for your good?" (Deuteronomy 10:12-13)

• "He has shown you, O man, what is good; and what does the Lord require of you but to do justly, to love mercy, and to walk humbly with your God?" (Micah 6:8)

• "'You shall love the Lord your God with all your heart, with all your soul, with all your strength, and with all your mind,' and 'your neighbor as yourself.'" (Luke 10:27)

---

[40] Frederick W. Faber, "The Right Must Win," 1849.

• "Moreover it is required in stewards that one be found faithful." (1 Corinthians 4:2)

What does it mean to be faithful? The *Oxford Dictionary* defines "faithful" as "loyal, constant (to a person or to one's word), conscientious, trustworthy." Nowadays, faithfulness is something that is much needed. But it does bring a reward. In Revelation 2:10, God says, "Be faithful until death, and I will give you the crown of life." This was said in connection with persecution, but I wonder if it is just as difficult to be faithful when things are going well with us.

We should pray that God will open our eyes to see and understand the promises contained in the Bible and that we will realize the power and life that are available to us if we have faith enough—and are willing to take the time—to use it.

Candles and Lamps[41]
John 1:1-12, Matthew 5:13-16

There used to be a special day called Church Candle Day, when a church was lit entirely by tallow candles, with each family contributing an equal share of the light.

When the electricity goes out, people get out their oil lamps to provide light. Let us consider the subject of lamps. In Matthew 5:16, we read, "Let your light so shine before men, that they may see your good works and glorify your Father in heaven." In what ways are we like lamps?

1. Lamps need to be tended and cared for—and used.

A lamp is of no value in itself. It can only shine when it is properly cared for and filled with oil. For best results, you need to clean the chimney, trim the wick, and fill the lamp with oil. Similarly, our lives need to be cared for, if we are to give light.

---

[41] This is an extended version of a devotional first delivered at Mission Circle in 1948.

We need keep our lives clean and pure. We need to trim away selfishness and indifference and other impurities. But, most importantly, to give light, we must be filled with the love of God and the power of His Spirit. Just as it is necessary for the wick to be in contact with the oil, so we must keep in touch with God through Bible study and prayer. Even electric light fixtures are useless unless they are connected to the source of power.

2. The main purpose of a lamp is to give light.

A lamp may be beautiful, but if it does not give light, it is of no value. A fancy light might not shine as brightly as a plainer one. Yet, in daylight, it is hard to tell. The test is when darkness arises. When we come out of the darkness into a lighted room, we do not notice the lamp but the light coming from it. Philip Brooks prized a letter that he had received. It said: "Dear Mr. Brooks: I am a tailor in a little shop near your church. When I have the opportunity, I always go to hear you preach. Each time I hear you, I seem to forget all about you, for you make me think of God." Do we live in such a way that people forget about us, see the light, and think of God?

3. There are many kinds of lamps, each for a different purpose.

There are hanging lamps to light a room, table lamps, plain lamps to give light for reading, and small lamps to guide us from room to room. In the same way, we all have our own place to shine, our own purpose in life. John Oxenham wrote:

Is your place a small place?
Tend it with care.
He set you there.
Is your place a large place?
Guard it with care!
He set you there.
Whatever your place, it is
Not yours alone, but His
Who set you there.

Annie Johnson Flint had many trials in her life. She was an invalid and very poor. We might think she would not have much opportunity for giving light, but she wrote many inspirational poems, including this one:

His lamp am I, to shine where He shall say,
And lamps are not for sunny rooms
Nor for the light of day,
But for the dark places of the earth
Where shame and crime and wrong have birth,
Or for the murky twilight gray
Where wandering sheep have gone astray,
Or where the light of faith grows dim
And souls are groping after Him.
And as sometimes a flame we find
Clear shining through the night,
So bright we do not see the lamp
But only see the light—
So may I shine, His light the flame,
That men may glorify His name.

Knowing God Better[42]

2 Kings 6:8-18 tells the story of the king of Syria sending his army to capture the prophet Elisha in the city of Dothan. When he saw the army surrounding the city, Elisha's servant was terrified. But Elisha said, "Do not fear, for those who are with us are more than those who are with them." Then Elisha prayed that God would open the servant's eyes, and the servant saw that "the mountain was full of horses and chariots of fire all around Elisha." It is important that God opens our eyes so that we will know better who God is.

1. God is Ruler over all.

That is, we need to recognize that God is in control.

---

[42] Prayer meeting, 1987. Besides morning and evening Sunday services, Waterford Baptist Church held a weekly prayer meeting on Wednesday evenings.

King Ahab was ruler over the northern kingdom of Israel. He brought in the worship of pagan idols, put the prophets of Baal on the government payroll, and persecuted the prophets of the true God so that 150 of them had to hide out in a cave. God could have destroyed Ahab, but he decided to give the king one more chance to change his ways. 1 Kings 17 tells how God sent the prophet Elijah to tell Ahab, "There shall not be dew nor rain these years, except at my word" (verse 1). God sent Elijah to hide out in the Cherith valley, and when the brook there dried up, he sent Elijah to live with a widow in Zarephath (in the pagan area from which Ahab had imported idol worship). The widow's son died, but when Elijah prayed, God restored him to life. Through all of this, Elijah and the widow were taught to trust God. Note that twice in this chapter, God said, "I have commanded..."—"the ravens to feed you" and "a widow to provide for you" (1 Kings 17: 4,9). Ahab thought he was the ruler of Israel, but it was God who was giving the orders.

2. God is mightier than all.

In accordance with Elijah's prophecy, there was no rain on the land for three-and-a-half years. 1 Kings 18 tells how Elijah defeated the 450 prophets of Baal and 400 prophets of Asherah on Mount Carmel, when the true God sent down fire to burn Elijah's sacrifice and the false prophets could not get Baal to answer. The people were convinced by this and said, "The Lord, He is God! The Lord, He is God!" (1 Kings 18:39). God then sent heavy rain, and Elijah ran ahead of Ahab's chariot all the way to the town of Jezreel.

3. God is with me.

In Exodus 33:14, God promised his people: "My Presence will go with you, and I will give you rest."

Sometimes the worst depressions come after the greatest victories. 1 Kings 19 tells us that after Elijah's victory on Mount Carmel, Queen Jezebel vowed to kill him. Elijah became depressed and ran away. He wanted to die. As he slept under a juniper tree, an angel woke him and showed him a fire, cakes, and water. He ate, slept, and ate again. Then he travelled for forty days south to Mount Horeb. God asked him, "What are you doing here, Elijah?" There was a violent wind, and earthquake, and fire, but God spoke to Elijah in "a still small voice" (1 Kings 19:9-12). God said that He still had work for Elijah to do. He told him to anoint Jehu as the new king of Israel. He told Elijah to anoint Elisha to take his place as prophet. And he told Elijah that there were still 7,000 people in Israel who had not bowed down and worshipped Baal.

4. God knows all.

1 Kings 21 tells the story of Queen Jezebel and King Ahab conspiring to have a man named Naboth killed so that Ahab could steal the man's vineyard. They got away with it. But then God sent Elijah to condemn Ahab and Jezebel for their crime. In 1 Chronicles 28:9 King David advised his son Solomon to serve God wholeheartedly because "the Lord searches all hearts and understands all the intent of the thoughts."

5. God's will is sovereign.

In 2 Kings 2, Elijah was about to be taken up to heaven and asked his successor Elisha what he would like. Elisha replied, "Please let a double portion of your spirit be upon me" (verse 9). Elijah replied that this great request would be granted only "if you see me when I am taken from you" (verse 10). Elisha needed to have faith enough to accept Elijah's statement. Elisha watched and saw Elijah taken up to heaven without dying, just as Enoch had been (Genesis 5:24). Then, Elisha's request was granted.

6. God is all-sufficient.

God was able to meet all of the needs of both Elijah and Elisha. In 2 Kings 2:19-22, Elisha changed bitter water into drinkable water. In 2 Kings 4:8-37, Elisha raised a dead boy to life. In 2 Kings 4:42-44, Elisha fed 100 hungry people with 20 loaves of bread and some grain, with some left over. In 2 Kings 6:1-7, Elisha made a lost iron ax head float on water, recovering it.

7. God is Ruler of the nations.

In 2 Kings 6-7, the Syrians kept invading Israel, but God warned the Israelites through Elisha where the invading armies would be so they could remain safe. The king of Syria then sent an army to kill Elisha. When the army surrounded the city where Elisha was, Elisha's servant was terrified. This was when Elisha said, "Do not fear, for those who are with us are more than those who are with them" (2 Kings 6:16) and Elisha asked God to open the servant's eyes and see the fiery horses and chariots of God's much greater army surrounding the enemy. God then deluded the Syrian army, allowing the whole army to be captured without any human force at all.

It is important that God opens our eyes so that we will know better who God is.

Paying Taxes

In Mark 12:13-17, some Pharisees and Herodians came to Jesus and asked, "Is it lawful to pay taxes to Caesar, or not?" The Pharisees did not like paying these taxes but did not outright oppose them. The Zealots were militant opponents of Rome and opposed paying these taxes. The Herodians (who supported the Roman-appointed ruler King Herod) supported paying the taxes.

Jesus asked to see a coin (with Caesar's image on it) and responded, "Render to Caesar the things that are Caesar's, and to God the things that are God's." We bear God's image. We were made in the image of God (Genesis 1:26), and so we should give Him what belongs to Him—our hearts. If we give Jesus priority, we can then fulfill our other responsibilities. We must do everything in the proper order.

Sadducees, Scribes, and a Poor Widow

In Mark 12:18-44, Jesus encountered three groups of people.

First, the Sadducees asked Jesus a trick question about a woman who was married to seven brothers who all died in succession, asking which one would be married to her in heaven. The Sadducees did not believe in the resurrection (life after death) or in angels or demons and did not expect a Messiah to come. Jesus answered their real question (about whether there is life after death). He pointed out that God had told Moses, "I am the God of Abraham, the God of Isaac, and the God of Jacob" (Exodus 3:6, Mark 12:26); since these men were already dead by then and God "is not the God of the dead, but the God of the living," this meant that there must be life after death. God had already promised in the Old Testament, "For behold, I create new heavens and a new earth; and the former shall not be remembered or come to mind" (Isaiah 65:17). The apostle Paul later affirmed that "we should not trust in ourselves but in God who raises the dead" (2 Corinthians 1:9). This is good news for us, but was it bad news for the Sadducees?

The scribes (teachers of the Old Testament law) then asked Jesus which was the first (or most important) commandment. Jesus answered, "The first of all the commandments is: 'Hear, O Israel, the Lord our God, the Lord is one. And you shall love the Lord your God with all your heart, with all your soul, with all your mind, and with all your strength.' This is the first commandment. And the second, like it, is this: 'You shall love your neighbor as yourself.' There is no other commandment greater than these" (Mark 12:29-31). Jesus then quoted a verse from David in the Old Testament showing that He (Jesus) was greater than David and was in fact God (Psalm 110:1, Mark 12:36). Jesus thus demonstrated that

74

He had a greater understanding of the Old Testament than the scribes, who were supposed to be the experts. Jesus then went on to condemn the scribes as hypocrites because they pretended to be godly while acting cruelly to poor widows.

Finally, Jesus encountered a poor widow (the kind of person the scribes oppressed), who made a tiny donation at the temple (Mark 12:41-44). In contrast to the Sadducees and scribes, Jesus praised her because she had given her whole livelihood (her whole life) to God.

The Destruction of the Temple

As they were leaving the temple in Jerusalem one day, one of Jesus' disciples exclaimed, "Teacher, see what manner of stones and what buildings are here!" (Mark 13:1). Jesus answered, "Do you see these great buildings? Not one stone shall be left upon another, that shall not be thrown down." Then Jesus launched into a series of near and distant prophecies, prophecies that would be fulfilled in a short time and prophecies that would not be fulfilled for thousands of years.

This temple was called Herod's temple because King Herod had planned and funded it. Reconstruction of the temple (to replace the small temple that had been erected after Judah's return from exile in Babylon) started in 19 BC and was finally completed in 64 AD. It was a magnificent structure built with stones one metre (three feet) high and five metres (fifteen feet) long. In fulfillment of Jesus' prophecy, it was destroyed by the Romans in 70 AD.

After the Israelites were freed from slavery in Egypt, God led them in the form of a cloud by day and a fire by night. He ordered them to build a tabernacle, a large tent. "The cloud of the Lord was above the tabernacle by day, and fire was over it by night," and "the glory of the Lord filled the tabernacle" (Exodus 40:34-38). In other words, God's presence was in the tabernacle. After they had entered the Promised Land, God ordered the Israelites to build the temple in Jerusalem to serve as God's "dwelling place," the place where God would be among human beings. But John 1:14 says that "The Word became flesh and dwelt among us, and we beheld His glory." That is, when Jesus came to earth, God was no longer present in the temple but in the person of Jesus. The temple in Jerusalem was no longer needed and was destroyed. But after Jesus had been crucified and resurrected, He ascended back into heaven (Acts 1:9-11). Where did God dwell among humans after that? In 1 Corinthians 3:16, Paul said to the Corinthian Christians, "Do you not know that you are the temple of God and that the Spirit of God dwells in you?" Paul repeated in 2 Corinthians 6: "You are the temple of the living God. As God has said: 'I will dwell in them and walk among them. I will be their God, and they shall be My people.'" In Ephesians 2:19-22, Paul described Christians as "being fitted together" and growing "into a holy temple in the Lord...a dwelling place of God in the Spirit." In other words, individual Christians are like stones put together in the church to serve as God's temple on earth. In Revelation, John was given a vision of the "new Jerusalem," heaven. He said, "But I saw no temple in it, for the Lord God Almighty and the Lamb are its temple" (Revelation 21:22).

Job

Like Proverbs, Ecclesiastes, and the Song of Solomon, Job is "wisdom literature." Wisdom is having experience or knowledge together with the power of being able to apply it critically or practically.

Job deals with questions of suffering, particularly the question "Why would a righteous God allow so much evil?" It deals with the "sovereignty of God" and "questions of God." Job is not so much about suffering as it is about God's sovereignty and wisdom.

Job is said to be "righteous." This means just, upright, virtuous, and law-abiding in regard to the relationship between God and man or between man and man, having a correct relationship to the will of God.

Job may be the earliest book of the Bible, written perhaps in the time of Abraham. Job probably lived before Moses since he acted as a priest to his family (Job 1:5). Job could mean "persecuted one" (in Hebrew) or "repentant one" (in Arabic). He lived in Uz, which was southeast of the Dead Sea.

Job was very rich. He had seven sons, three daughters, 7,000 sheep, 3,000 camels, 500 yoke of oxen, 500 female donkeys, and many servants.

In Job 1:6-12, Satan came with the sons of God (angels) to challenge God. Satan is a fallen angel and is "the adversary" or "the accuser" who wants to attack God's people (1 Peter 5:8, Revelation 12:7-10). But Satan cannot attack without God's permission: "The angel of the Lord encamps all around those who fear Him, and delivers them" (Psalm 34:7). Satan's attack was not so much against Job as against God, Satan and the forces of evil fighting against God and the forces of righteousness.

Job was robbed of all his property (Job 1:13-22), and Job exhibited several signs of mourning (verse 20). Is it wrong to mourn? Verse 22 says, "In all this Job did not sin."

In chapter 2, Satan attacked Job's health. Being covered with boils would have been very itchy. Job's friends arrived and mourned with him (2:11-13). In chapter 3, Job asked, "Why was I born?" (verse 10) and "Why didn't I die at birth?" (verse 11) He said that rich and poor are all alike at death (verses 11-20). Finally, he said, "The thing I greatly feared has come upon me" (verse 25).

Many treatments of the suffering of Job start with chapters 1-2 and then skip chapters 3-31. Job's friends sat on the ground with him for seven days and nights, but as soon as they opened their mouths, things went downhill fast. Job called them miserable comforters in Job 16:1.

In Job 4, Eliphaz said Job's troubles must be the result of sin—a man reaps what he sows. Because God is a just God, goodness is rewarded, and sin is punished in this life. In 4:14-17, he recalled a nightmare when a spirit said this. In chapter 5, Eliphaz called Job foolish—implying that he had brought this trouble on himself by not humbling himself.

In chapter 6, Job lost his temper and attacked his friends. In chapter 7, he turned his complaints toward God.

In chapter 8, Bildad the Shuhite told Job his words were like a strong wind (verse 2), that Job's children were punished for their sins (verse 4), and that if Job would repent, God would restore his prosperity.

In chapter 9, Job described God's majesty and power over nature and wished for a mediator (verses 32-33). We now know that mediator is Jesus Christ. In chapter 10, Job pleaded his own case. He asked why God would want to destroy him after going to all the trouble of creating him (verses 18-22).

In chapter 11, Zophar the Naamathite also blamed Job, saying that if Job were really righteous, he would not be suffering, but if he repented of his sins, God would end his suffering.

In chapter 12, Job answered his critics (sarcastically) and spoke of the greatness of God. In Chapter 13, Job said he was not inferior to his friends and went directly to God to plead his case. He affirmed, "Though He slay me, yet will I trust Him" (verse 15). In chapter 14, Job discussed the frailty of life and again hoped for death.

What can we learn from all this? The answer is in an old poem:

Boys flying kites haul in their swift-winged birds.
It isn't that way when you're flying words.
Thoughts unexpressed fall back to earth dead,
But God Himself can't stop them once they're said.

Job was hurt by the words of his friends and his family (19:13-20). Jesus warned, "Judge not, that you be not judged" (Matthew 7:1-6). James advised, "So then, my beloved brethren, let every man be swift to hear, slow to speak, slow to wrath" (James 1:19).

Grief[43]

What does the Bible have to say about grief? In Lamentations 3:22-25,31-33, the prophet Jeremiah struggled with grief and clung to his faith in God in a difficult time:

Through the LORD's mercies we are not consumed,
Because His compassions fail not.
They are new every morning;
Great is Your faithfulness.
"The LORD is my portion," says my soul,
"Therefore I hope in Him!"
The LORD is good to those who wait for Him,
To the soul who seeks Him...
For the Lord will not cast off forever.
Though He causes grief,
Yet He will show compassion
According to the multitude of His mercies.
For He does not afflict willingly,
Nor grieve the children of men.

Psalm 30:5 says something similar: "Weeping may endure for a night, but joy comes in the morning."

Knowing this, what should our attitude be? These verses suggest some answers:

• "Now to Him who is able to do exceedingly abundantly above all that we ask or think, according to the power that works in

---

[43] These verses were recorded in Mom's notebook on July 3-4, 1991. Her husband, Ernie, was then in hospital and died on July 8. The later verses on God's presence were added September 15, 1991.

us, to Him be glory in the church by Christ Jesus to all generations, forever and ever. Amen" (Ephesians 3:20-21).

• Ephesians 5:20 says that we should be "giving thanks always for all things to God the Father in the name of our Lord Jesus Christ."

• Paul said that his goal was "that I may know Him and the power of His resurrection, and the fellowship of His sufferings" (Philippians 3:10). The thought of God's power and the promise of resurrection are encouraging, but what does it mean to share in Christ's suffering? Is it that we must experience death in order to have a share in the resurrection?

• Paul said that we should consider ourselves "bondservants of Christ, doing the will of God from the heart" (Ephesians 6:6).

In our grief, it is helpful to remember that God promises to remain with those who follow Him:

• "Let your conduct be without covetousness; be content with such things as you have. For He Himself has said, 'I will never leave you nor forsake you.' So we may boldly say: 'The Lord is my helper; I will not fear'" (Hebrews 13:5-6).

• God promised Jacob: "Behold, I am with you and will keep you wherever you go" (Genesis 28:15).

• Through Moses, God promised Joshua and the Israelites: "Be strong and of good courage, do not fear nor be afraid of them; for the Lord your God, He is the One who goes with you. He will not leave you nor forsake you...The Lord, He is the One who goes before you. He will be with you, He will not leave you nor forsake you; do not fear nor be dismayed" (Deuteronomy 31:6,8). God later directly affirmed this promise to Joshua: "As I was with Moses, so I will be with you. I will not leave you nor forsake you" (Joshua 1:5).

Lucky Are the Unlucky

Do the Beatitudes (Matthew 5:1-12) make sense today? The American dream is to reach a point in your life when you don't have to do anything you don't want to do and can do everything you want to do. The J.B. Phillips translation of Matthew 5 says, "How happy are..." But are millionaires happy? Are Lotto 649 winners happy? Are movie and TV stars happy?

Do we really want to take shortcuts? Jesus had been on "the other side." He knew all the glories of heaven, things so wonderful that "Eye has not seen, nor ear heard, nor have entered into the heart of man the things which God has prepared for those who love Him" (1 Corinthians 2:9). And yet He left them to come to earth to save us.

The Beatitudes are not a list of rules but a set of congratulations directed at those whose lives exemplify godly attitudes. The Ten Commandments are laws, telling us what we are not to do: "You shall not..." But in the Beatitudes Jesus illustrates the nature of God's will and deals with the thoughts and attitudes behind the actions. An attitude is a settled behaviour. An attitude of mind is a settled mode of thinking.

Let us look at the individual beatitudes:

Blessed are the poor in spirit. Who are the poor in spirit? People who are depressed, not very spiritual, oppressed, lonely, confused, needy. People who are poor in spirit recognize they have a need and are more likely to seek help and pray. They are the opposite of the people in Laodicea, who said, "I am rich, have become wealthy, and have need of nothing," and who did not know that they were "wretched, miserable, poor, blind, and naked" (Revelation 3:17).

Blessed are those who mourn, for they shall be comforted. The spiritual songs of black slaves were full of mourning, and yet the songs comforted the singers. We mourn at funerals, and yet we are blessed with the hope of seeing our loved ones again.

Blessed are the meek. These are people who are humble and submissive, such as Moses and Ruth and Mother Teresa and Martin Luther King.

Blessed are those who hunger and thirst for righteousness. These are people who are hungry and know they need filling, so they spend time in Bible study and prayer. They are the opposite of modern people who hunger and thirst for a good time and look out for number one.

Blessed are the merciful. These are people who extend forgiveness to others.

Blessed are the pure in heart. How do we keep our hearts pure? Philippians 4:8 gives one answer: "Whatever things are true, whatever things are noble, whatever things are just, whatever things are pure, whatever things are lovely, whatever things are of good report, if there is any virtue and if there is anything praiseworthy—meditate on these things." Ephesians 6:11-17 tell us to put on "the whole armor of God," and the next verse reminds us to pray always. 1 Corinthians 6:19 tells us to remember that we are "the temple of the Holy Spirit" and to act in keeping with that holy calling.

Blessed are the peacemakers, for they shall be called sons of God. There are pacifists, who refuse to fight, but we should be "pacificists," always seeking to bring peace. In a conflict, we should remember that there are two ways of looking at things. Therefore, we need to really listen and seek to understand others.

Blessed are those who are persecuted for righteousness' sake. I think of Norman Dabbs, a Canadian missionary to Bolivia who was murdered by a mob in 1949, and of missionary Jim Elliot and his four companions who were murdered in 1956 by the Auca native people in Ecuador whom they had gone to evangelize.

Jesus summed up the Beatitudes by saying, "You are the salt of the earth (a little scattered among many) and, "You are the light of the world" (Matthew 5:12-13). Jesus was speaking to His disciples. Jesus said, "I am the way, the truth, and the life. No one comes to the Father except through Me" (John 14:6). Those who enter God's kingdom must submit to God's rule. God provides those in his kingdom with the royal guidance and power to carry out these otherwise impossible demands. Paul advised Christians, "Let this mind be in you which was also in Christ Jesus" (Philippians 2:5) and then went on to describe how Jesus exemplified humility, obedience, and self-sacrifice, the same attitude Jesus taught in the Beatitudes.

Can You Sign up for Immortality?[44]

On the cover of the April 2 issue of *Maclean's* magazine, a heading caught my eye: "Freeze now—Live later! (Can you sign up for immortality?)" The article began with this sentence: "Someone somewhere will soon earn a place in the history of mankind by dying and then being instantly frozen solid, so that he can be stored in a freezer for a century or two in the hope scientists will learn how to bring him back alive." The writer went on to tell of the difficulties involved in freezing the body instantly before brain damage takes place, the problems of keeping the body frozen and intact, and the problems of storage. But, surprisingly enough, there are people who believe this can be done, and, according to a reporter, "about 20 new converts a week" are signing up with the movement started by a US physicist. There is even a branch of eight members in Montreal. They say they have not run into much opposition from religious groups. When asked by the writer why people would join a movement like this, one young woman answered, "One lifetime is hardly enough."

They do not know or do not realize that two thousand years ago Christ said, "He who believes in the Son has everlasting life" (John 3:36) and "I am the resurrection and the life. He who believes in Me, though he may die, he shall live.

---

[44] Mission Circle, April 27, 1966.

And whoever lives and believes in Me shall never die" (John 11:25-26).

The "Life Extension Society" movement sounds like something out of science fiction, and one wonders that anyone would get involved with it. But it does seem to illustrate the thinking of a large number of people today who seem to have lost belief in God. Life presents many problems, and, as professing Christians, we ask ourselves: "How can we meet this need?" We are surrounded by people who are dissatisfied with their lives, people who are discouraged, and modern people who feel that Christianity is old-fashioned and out of date. How can we convey to them the message that Christ is still alive—"the same yesterday, today, and forever" (Hebrews 13:8)—and that by faith in Him we have an answer to every problem.

Perhaps the first thing to consider is that we cannot pass on to others what we are not sure of ourselves. We have to possess a faith that will withstand the trials and temptations of life before we can pass it on. Then, too, we must be willing to become involved in the problems of others and be willing to share their burdens.

Perhaps, most of all, we need to consider the passage we read in Mark (1:16-20), where Jesus said to Peter and Andrew, "Follow Me, and I will make you become fishers of men" and then similarly called James and John to leave their nets and follow Him.

As we have fellowship with Christ and commit our way to Him, He will enable us to become His co-workers. Peter and Andrew and James and John did not become fishers of men immediately. Even after the ascension, the disciples had to wait another ten days until, at the time of Pentecost, they were given power.

We must also remember that if God has a task for us, He meets us on our own level, and He always starts with something we are able to do. Moses was asked, "What is that in your hand?" (Exodus 4:2) Moses learned that his shepherd's staff *plus God* was adequate for bringing the children of Israel out of Egypt. David had only a slingshot and five little stones, but with God's help they were enough to deliver Israel from Goliath. When Jesus fed the multitude, He asked the disciples, "How many loaves do you have?" (Mark 6:38). They reported that all they could find was five loaves and two fish, but these, broken and blessed by the Lord Jesus, were enough to feed five thousand, with twelve baskets left over. So, too, we find that our meagre resources and abilities, when dedicated to God and used by Him, are more than sufficient to meet every demand for strength and service.

We often repeat the Great Commission: "Go therefore and make disciples of all the nations" (Matthew 28:19). But we forget what precedes it and follows it: "All authority has been given to Me in heaven and on earth" and "Lo, I am with you always, even to the end of the age" (Matthew 28:18,20).

If we are willing to link our limited abilities with the limitless power of God, we will be able to do our part to meet the world's needs.

What Causes Worry?

In studying God's Word, we are amazed to discover that its teachings are just as up-to-date now as they were in Bible times. That is just another fact that helps to convince us that the Bible is God's Word. How many of the books written today will be used a hundred years from now? Yet the Bible never fails to meet our needs if we study it prayerfully.

Let us consider Matthew 6:25-34. Christ was warning His followers about spending their lives worrying about earthly matters. Instead, He said, "Seek first the kingdom of God and His righteousness" (Matthew 6:33).

In reading magazines and newspapers today, we often see articles written about the harm that worry can do to our bodies. People are beginning to learn that many diseases are caused or aggravated by worry or by the strain of modern life. No matter where we go, it seems that people are worried and fearful.

What causes this sense of worry?

1. Fear of the Future

A question troubling many people is whether there will be another war, and we are told of the dreadful things that will happen if it comes. We hear a great deal about the word "security." There are family allowances and old age pensions, and yet people still worry about the future. One remedy suggested for this is for us to just worry about one day at a time. We can't do our best work today if we are continually worrying about tomorrow. "For yesterday is but a dream, and tomorrow is only a vision. But today well lived makes every yesterday a dream of happiness and every tomorrow a vision of hope."

There will always be certain troubles which we cannot avoid, but it doesn't help to worry about them. No one escapes having some trouble.

In Luke 9:23 and Matthew 16:24, Jesus said, "If anyone desires to come after Me, let him deny himself, and take up his cross *daily*, and follow Me." In Matthew 6:11, He taught us to pray, "Give us this day our *daily* bread." This reminds us of God providing manna to the Israelites in the wilderness, but only enough for one day at a time.

2. Busyness

Another cause of worry in our lives is the feeling of having so many jobs to do that we don't know which one to do first. Everywhere we go, we hear people complaining that they haven't got enough time. Do we ever use lack of time as an excuse for something we do not want to do? Yet, as one person said to me, "There are just as many hours in a day as there ever were." Look at the conveniences and labour-saving devices we have today that our grandmothers lacked. But what do we do with the time we save? Have we lost the spirit of neighbourliness that seemed to prevail in pioneer days?

I once heard a sermon on the subject of time. The minister stressed the fact that there is time for everything we *really* want to do. He warned, "Don't let the things that matter be crowded out by the things that don't matter much."

If anyone came to seek Jesus' help, did He ever tell them He had no time? He was always ready to help someone, whether as He paused to rest by the well in Samaria or when Nicodemus came to Him by night. When the mothers brought the children to Him, He was ready to speak to them.

3. No Time for God

Another reason that we are worried and feel so rushed is that we have forgotten to pause for communion with God. Is that why some people are able to accomplish more than others in the same amount of time? If we pause for a few minutes for silent prayer or reading God's Word, we will go on our way refreshed and soon make up the time. After all, God is willing to help us bear our burdens. I Peter 5:7 tells us to cast "all your care upon Him, for He cares for you." In Matthew 10:29-31, Jesus assured His followers, "Are not two sparrows sold for a copper coin? And not one of them falls to the ground apart from your Father's will. But the very hairs of your head are all numbered. Do not fear therefore; you are of more value than many sparrows." Deuteronomy 33:25 assures us, "As your days, so shall your strength be."

4. Indecision

Finally, are any of us troubled by a lack of decision in our lives? Jesus said, "No one can serve two masters" (Matthew 6:24). If we make a decision for Him, we find it helps to solve other problems. Or perhaps we feel there is some task we should do for Him but we keep postponing it.

In the Bible, God has given us many wonderful promises, but in nearly all of them, there is a condition to be met. This is also true in today's passage (Matthew 6:25-34). Jesus assured us, "Your heavenly Father knows that you need all these things" and promised, "All these things shall be added to you" (Matthew 6:32-33). But don't forget the condition: "Seek first the kingdom of God and His righteousness" (Matthew 6:33). Are we putting His kingdom first? If we do, we need have no fear of the future.

What Are You Looking For?[45]

Jesus told the parable of the lost coin (Luke 15:8-10) and the parable of the hidden treasure (Matthew 13:44). Everyone is searching for something in life—money, fame, happiness...Perhaps everyone is really looking for happiness and trying to attain it in various ways, some through fame and some through riches.

Here is what the Bible says about searching:
• "You will seek Me and find Me, when you search for Me with all your heart" (Jeremiah 29:13).
• "Without faith it is impossible to please Him, for he who comes to God must believe that He is, and that He is a rewarder of those who diligently seek Him" (Hebrews 11:6).
• "Seek first the kingdom of God and His righteousness, and all these things shall be added to you" (Matthew 6:33).
• "Ask, and it will be given to you; seek, and you will find; knock, and it will be opened to you" (Matthew 7:7).
• "O God, You are my God; early will I seek You" (Psalm 63:1).
• "Seek Me and live" (Amos 5:4).
• "The Son of Man has come to seek and to save that which was lost" (Luke 19:10).
Just as everyone is looking for something, so God is seeking us too. He wants our friendship and love.

---

[45] Goodwill Bible Class, September 4, 1972.

What Are You Searching for?[46]

Amos 5:4,6,8,14-15, Jeremiah 29:10-13, Matthew 13:44-46

All of these passages tell us to seek God.

For what are you searching? I imagine it would be very difficult to find any person who is absolutely contented with his life. Everyone seems to be searching for something—money, popularity, or fame—and by these various routes they all hope to attain the same goal of happiness.

Life tends to get rather monotonous at times, and occasionally I find myself envious of those who travel to far-off places and wishing I had a chance to see some of those exotic spots.

Last week, in a magazine, I happened to see a prayer by Marjorie Holmes which really seemed to express my feelings. She began by thanking God for her home and family and husband and said she should be content with her blessings. But she kept wishing that something exciting would happen and that some glamorous movie star or foreign diplomat might drop in for a visit. But, instead of a foreign diplomat, an oil truck backed into the driveway with fuel for the furnace, and the milkman brought milk for breakfast. She realized that these were necessities and perhaps the oil man was more important to her well-being than the foreign diplomat. However, the longing for something more persisted, and she realized that perhaps this longing had been placed in her heart by God so that she would never be satisfied with mere existence but would be always trying to enrich her life by means of great paintings, literature, music, or travel. Man does not live by bread alone (Deuteronomy 8:3, Matthew 4:4).

---

[46] September 1972. This meditation was likely delivered to the Mission Circle. Mom and Dad took a trip to northern Ontario September 9-12, 1972.

Last week, we had a chance to enrich our lives through a trip to northern Ontario. Miss Pearce[47] phoned me a day or so before we left and asked me to help with the program. Before we left, I glanced over some ideas and references I had compiled on "seeking God," and on the trip these seemed to keep popping up in my mind. Our objective when we set out was to see places we had never visited. We had been to Sudbury and New Liskeard, but this time we took the northern of the two routes through northern Ontario. I found many parallels between our trip and the spiritual seeking we have been reading about. We had a car in good condition (faith), gas (prayer), food (the Bible), and accommodations (the house of God). There are other parallels with biblical journeys.

1. The Importance of Side Trips

On our trip, we made side trips to interesting sites. In the Coniston/Wanup area, we saw where they had blasted a road through a massive hill and also a remarkable suspension bridge. At Sault Ste. Marie, we saw the two-mile-long international bridge. At Wawa, we saw the Scenic High Falls on the Magpie River. This reminded me of Exodus 3:2-3, where Moses "turned aside" to see the burning bush and met God. In Mark 6:31, when the disciples were exhausted from their ministry trip and distracted by the hustle and bustle going on around them, Jesus told them, "Come aside by yourselves to a deserted place and rest a while."

2 Seeking Requires Persistence.

We encountered many magnificent views of Lake Superior, rock cuts, and high rounded hills. We kept turning into picnic areas and scenic lookouts to take pictures. Unfortunately, there were many trucks (it was the Trans-Canada Highway) and had difficulties trying to pass them.

---

[47] Home missionary Marion Pearce had worked as a social worker in Toronto with many new Canadians arriving after the First World War and later taught Latin at Waterford District High School. She was an active member of Waterford Baptist Church and president of the mission circle from 1946 to 1966.

Sometimes we would come to the top of a long hill, and there would be magnificent view of valleys and the road winding around another hill many miles ahead or a glimpse of Lake Superior. We would have liked to have stopped to take a picture, but to stop might have caused an accident. In life, sometimes perhaps we stand still and dream of the future, or perhaps, as we grow older, we stand on the hilltop and look back at the past, which seems to improve with distance, instead of keeping on with our journey.

One spectacular scenic lookout was at Little Pic River near Marathon. We couldn't help wondering as we drove along what mighty forces had been at work in the far distant past to shape those rocks. We couldn't help admiring the knowledge and courage of those who had cut the course of the railway and roads through those rocks many years ago. And there were historical plaques for the fur traders who had journeyed through this area even earlier.

3. Seeking Requires Patience.

We found patience was required on the northern route of the Trans-Canada Highway. There was magnificent scenery between Nipigon and Beardmore. There were high cliffs along the rivers. We saw log booms and logging trucks. The gold-mining towns of Beardmore and Geraldton were interesting. But the road was inclined to be a bit monotonous—a long, straight road between birch and spruce forests, with only occasional low hills, a few rocks, little traffic, and not many leaves turning colour yet.

4. There Are Compensations along the Way.

We gained some idea of the vastness of our province. Ten miles west of Geraldton, we came to the Arctic Divide—from this point on, all streams flow north to the Arctic Ocean. We encountered another divide thirty miles south of Matheson—from this point south all streams flow into the Atlantic Ocean. We saw the Trans-Canada Pipeline. We saw Canada jays, chipmunks, and a moose crossing area. We saw great contrasts—forest, towns, cemeteries, and farming country—

as well as the differences between Ontario and Quebec. After we reached Matheson, we realized it was time to turn toward home again, ready for work once again. We had an increased realization of the blessings we have received.

5. Jesus Is also Concerned with Seeking.

In Luke 19:10, Jesus said, "The Son of Man has come to seek and to save that which was lost." In Matthew 6:33, Jesus taught us: "Seek first the kingdom of God and His righteousness, and all these things shall be added to you."

The Great Highway[48]
Isaiah 35

As we think back over our experiences of the past summer, most of us can recall some pleasant trip that we have taken. Associated with these memories are those of the roads over which we have travelled to reach our destination. There are such a variety of them, from busy highways to quiet, winding roads through the woods or beside some distant lake. Roads seem to play such an important part in our modern life, and our governments seem to be continually building wider and better ones.

But, beyond all the roads that man has made and infinitely far surpassing them is the great road that God has made for His people: "A highway shall be there, and a road, and it shall be called the Highway of Holiness" (Isaiah 35:8). Let us take this text as a parable of the Christian life, a picture of the road along which the feet of God's folk are forever travelling. There are four features of the road mentioned in the text.

1. A High Way

Every one of us in our passage through the world is confronted by two ways, a high way and a low way, and is

---

[48] Ladies Aid, September 9, 1954.

compelled to make a choice between them. This was clearly expressed in a poem by John Oxenham:

To every man there openeth
A Way, and Ways, and a Way.
And the High Soul climbs the High way,
And the Low Soul gropes the Low,
And in between, on the misty flats,
The rest drift to and fro.
But to every man there openeth
A High Way, and a Low.
And every man decideth
The Way his soul shall go.[49]

The human soul seems to be forever coming to another fork where the two roads divide. The tragedy is that so many take the wrong road. Large numbers of them think it is the true way and keep going along it, hoping everything will turn out alright in the end. But in Proverbs 14:12 we read: "There is a way that seems right to a man, but its end is the way of death." Every way which is not God's way for us is no way at all. Either it will turn out to be a dead end road, or it will lead us miles from our destination. Just as we have guidebooks and maps to show us which route to take on the highway, so, too, we have God's guidebook, the Bible, to tell us which path to take along God's Highway. Then, too, as we pass over a strange road, we anxiously look for signs pointing to our destination. Are we looking as eagerly for God's signposts to make sure we are on God's Highway?

2. A Harmless Way

God's Highway, too, is a harmless way. It is strange, perhaps, to find savage monsters such as lions, tigers, and leopards in God's fair world. But these also have their counterparts in the moral world. There are fierce temptations that leap out upon us when we least suspect their presence and seem ready to destroy our souls. We have all met temptations

---

[49] "The Ways" by William Arthur Dunkerley (1852-1941), writing as John Oxenham.

like these. But God says: "No lion shall be there, nor shall any ravenous beast go up on it" (Isaiah 35:9). That does not say that they may not come near the Highway, but there is always a safe way through for those who lead a holy life. In John Bunyan's *The Pilgrim's Progress*, when Christian is climbing the Hill Difficulty, he remembers that Timorous and Mistrust warned him that there were ravenous lions there. But a porter named Watchful assured him, "Fear not the lions; for they are chained...keep in the midst of the path, and no hurt shall come unto thee!"[50]

3. A Happy Way

Next, we are told it is a happy way. Nowadays, people seem to consider that happiness is an elemental human right, and a great many of them seem to require a multitude of material possessions to keep them happy. But the fact is that we cannot enjoy ourselves in the highest sense unless we enjoy God. He is the source of every true happiness, and the way He bids us journey is a way of joy. So many people seem to take it for granted that the people travelling God's way all wear long faces, and they never bother trying His way to find out for themselves. Certainly, the people in this text were not sad: "And the ransomed of the Lord shall return, and come to Zion with singing, with everlasting joy on their heads. They shall obtain joy and gladness, and sorrow and sighing shall flee away" (Isaiah 35:10).

4. A Homeward Way

Last of all, this road we are speaking of is the homeward way. Every road is good, however rough and steep and winding, if it leads home at last. There is no doubt that this royal road leads home at last. For centuries, it has been trodden by the feet of countless travellers, and no one who has taken it has failed to find the open door and the light burning in the window at the end.

---

[50] John Bunyan (1628-1688), *The Pilgrim's Progress*, 1678.

Let us tonight take another look about us and make sure that we are travelling God's Highway and that our feet are still on the right pathway.

What Do We See?[51]
Psalm 24:1-5

In some ways, September is like New Year's. So many people and organizations seem to make a fresh start then. As fall approaches, we find ourselves looking backward at summer and vacation time and looking forward with renewed energy to the tasks that lie ahead.

Probably at some time during the summer, most of us have had some opportunity to travel about the countryside, whether the trip was long or short. As we travel about or as we stay at home, just *what do we see?* Are we like David in Psalm 33:5, conscious of the fact that "the earth is full of the goodness of the Lord"?

In searching for a suitable Scripture passage to talk about today, I started reading the Psalms and was amazed at the number of them that are praising God for His goodness:

• "The heavens declare the glory of God" (Psalm 19:1).

• "Bless the Lord, O my soul" (Psalm 103:1).

• In Psalm 116:12, David asks, "What shall I render to the Lord for all His benefits toward me?"

When travelling on some of the highways in northern Ontario, one occasionally comes to a sign announcing a "lookout station" ahead. If one takes the trouble to stop, one is usually able to obtain a magnificent view of the surrounding countryside. Even at home, do we not need to pause occasionally and look about us at all of the benefits we enjoy?

While on a vacation trip to northern Ontario this summer, we happened to meet a relative from this district, and of course

---

[51] September 8, 1955.

we began to compare notes on the routes we had taken. We asked him if he had passed through a certain town, and he replied, "I don't know. I was driving so fast I'm not sure of what towns we went through." That is probably the experience of a lot of people nowadays, and I don't imagine that anyone travelling on these new superhighways would have much time to slow down and admire the view and think about the goodness of God.

But these things are all there if we only have eyes to see them. Most of us are familiar with this poem:

Two men looked out from prison bars.
One saw mud, the other saw stars.

We usually see what we are looking for.

When one thinks of the innumerable ways in which God has provided for His people, how can anyone doubt that there is a God? Even in our own province, Giod has given us choice of a great variety of occupations. In travelling about, one sees the Great Lakes with their sandy beaches and their fisheries. There are the rich farming lands in this district, the orchards of the Niagara district, and the market gardens of the Holland Marsh. Farther north, there is the wealth of the forests and the mines. No one but God could have planned anything like this.

Do you recall the story of the transfiguration? Do you remember how Peter wanted to stay on the mountaintop? But, instead, Jesus took them back down the mountainside to where the multitudes were awaiting His help.

If we will only pause once in a while to appreciate the wonderful things with which God has surrounded us, perhaps we, too, will catch a glimpse of the glory of God and then will be better prepared to go out and serve Him faithfully. Let us tonight pause and consider God's goodness to us and then ask ourselves as David did, "What shall I render to the Lord for all His benefits toward me?"

What Do You Have in the House?[52]

2 Kings 4:1-7

This passage tells the story of the widow of a prophet who came to Elisha and said that she was in debt and her sons were about to be sold into slavery. Elisha asked, "What do you have in the house?" She replied that she had only a jar of oil. He told her to borrow as many containers as she could and pour oil from her jar into the containers. When the oil filled all the containers, Elisah told her to sell the oil, pay her debts with the money she received, and live on the rest of the money. There are several key aspects of this story which are relevant for us.

1. Faith

The woman did what Elisha told her to do. Would we have carried out an instruction like that, an instruction that must have seemed strange and even ridiculous? Do we have as much faith as this woman?

2. Ask

The woman received according to her faith. All the containers that she borrowed were filled. Should she have borrowed more? Do we ask enough of God? Missionary William Carey said, "Expect great things from God. Attempt great things for God."

3. Work

The woman had to supply the jar of oil. God can and will do wonderful things, but we must also make our contribution. God gives the harvest, but men must plant the seed. In the miracles of Jesus, the recipients had to do their part:

• Jesus miraculously fed five thousand people, but His followers had to first contribute five loaves and two fishes (Matthew 14:13-21).

---

[52] Nancy Mitchell Mission Circle, September 1962.

• Jesus healed a man with a withered hand, but first Jesus told him to "Stretch out your hand" (Matthew 12:9-14).

• Jesus healed a man with an infirmity by the pool of Bethesda but only as he obeyed Jesus' command to "Rise, take up your bed and walk" (John 5:1-9).

In the Parable of the Talents, Jesus said that God rewarded those who invested their talents (Matthew 24:14-30). God does not want your money; He wants you! Why shouldn't we sow our talents as we sow seed?

The Life of A.V. Timpany[53]

Americus Vespucius Timpany (1840-1885) was a Canadian missionary to India. He was named after Amerigo Vespucci, a European explorer whose name was given to the Americas.

The American Baptist Missionary Union established a mission in India in 1835, sending a Canadian, Rev. S.S. Day, to start the work. He was joined in 1848 by Rev. Lyman Jewith. In the first eighteen years, they gained only five converts, but they persevered, and the results improved. In 1866, twenty-eight converts were baptized in a single day.

A.V. Timpany was born in Calton in Elgin County, Ontario, in 1840. He attended Sunday school and church. He heard about the missionaries who had gone to India and wanted to help. His father suggested he plant an apple tree. After the last spadefull of soil had been smoothed down, he straightened up and said, "There! That's my foreign missionary tree." When the tree bore fruit, the apples were sold and the money given to missions.

---

[53] Mission Band, March 1971. Mission Band was a club for children designed to inform them about Christian missions. The children's Sunday school classes in Waterford Baptist Church were named after missionaries; one of them was named after A.V. Timpany.

Some years afterward, A.V. felt God wanted him to be a missionary. One day, he went back to the woods, sat on a log, and thought things out. He felt that God was saying to him, "Leave all and follow Me." He was a Christian and wanted to love and serve Christ, but he also liked his home farm and family and didn't want to leave them. Then he thought of the heathen world that he had heard about. How terrible it would be if God wanted him there! He could see the farm and his apple tree and thought how hard it would be to go away. But finally he decided that if God wanted him to be a missionary, he would go.

A.V. enrolled at a Baptist college in Woodstock, Ontario, in 1860 and graduated in 1866. The Baptists of Ontario wished to send a missionary under the American Baptist Missionary Union, and A.V. volunteered to go.

When he came back to his own church to preach his farewell sermon, the church building couldn't hold all the people who wanted to come, and the service was held in a pine grove with about 2,000 people present.

A.V. didn't go alone. When he was attending college, he met the daughter of a minister in Woodstock. Her name was Jane Bates, and her family was very interested in missions. A.V. and Jane were married in 1867, the year of Canada's Confederation. There were many preparations to be made for the trip. Women in India wore saris, and when lady missionaries went to India, they took enough clothes to last for many years. Jane's family were not rich, and the ladies of the churches volunteered to supply her clothes. They got busy and made a good supply. Ladies from Brantford were leaders in this.

On October 17, 1867, the Baptist convention was held in Woodstock, and A.V. and his wife were appointed to the work in India. A.V. spoke, and then a collection was taken. They were still short about fifty dollars of the amount they needed. People started bringing gifts. They kept coming and coming until in a little over an hour $1,152 were collected.

In October, A.V. and Jane sailed from New York to England and then south around the Cape of Good Hope (southern Africa) in a sailing ship to India. Two Telegu women accompanied them and taught them the language on the way. They reached Madras, India, on April 15,1868. They then had to travel 108 miles to Nellore. Jane travelled in a palanquin (a box suspended on one or two poles and carried by four to six men). A.V. travelled in an oxcart, which averaged two miles an hour. They were on the road for five nights. After two more years of language study, they moved to Ramapatnam with their infant son. Seventy converts were baptized that year.

In October 1869, John McLaurin (from the Ottawa area) and Mary Bates (Jane's sister) were married, and they went to India to help the Timpanys. The church ladies made clothes for Mary as they had for Jane. Mr. and Mrs. McLaurin sailed from New York via the Suez Canal[54], arriving in Madras on February 12, 1870.

In 1874, the McLaurins moved to Cocanada. In 1875, they were joined by other missionaries from Nova Scotia, bringing dried apples from Canada. By 1876, two churches had been organized, ten chapels/schools had been built, and a theological seminary had been established to train Indian pastors.

Mr. and Mrs. Timpany came home on furlough in 1876 and then moved to Cocanada on their return to India. A new church and a girls' boarding school were built.

On February 19, 1885, A.V. rose as usual, but by 8:00 a.m. he was not feeling well. At 2:30 p.m., he died of cholera, probably contracted by drinking unpasteurized milk offered to him while he was on a trip a day or two before. The Timpanys' two older children were in Canada then. Daughter Mary was at school in the city but was not able to get home in time to say goodbye to her father. The funeral was at 9:00 p.m. A.V.'s body was carried in a torchlight procession through the town and

---

[54] Construction of the Suez Canal had just been finished. It was officially opened on November 17, 1869.

across the river to the cemetery. His wife, Jane Timpany, returned to Canada, but two of their children later returned to India as missionaries.

Decisions
Matthew 7:13-14

Life is made up of decisions—what to wear, what to eat, whether to sit and watch TV or to do something worthwhile.

Jesus talked about an important decision that is laid before each one of us: "Enter by the narrow gate; for wide is the gate and broad is the way that leads to destruction, and there are many who go in by it. Because narrow is the gate and difficult is the way which leads to life, and there are few who find it" (Matthew 7:13-14). In commenting on this verse, a pastor said that the gate is so narrow that there is only room for one person to pass through it at a time. We all have to make this decision on our own.

Other passages in the Bible also talk about choosing to enter through that narrow gate and follow God's way:

• Revelation 3:7 says that Jesus is "He who opens and no one shuts, and shuts and no one opens." Jesus has control of opening and closing gates.

• In Zechariah 3:7, God promises that if we commit ourselves to walking in His ways, "I will give you places to walk."

• In Isaiah 58:13-14, God promises that if we choose to honour Him and delight in Him, "I will cause you to ride on the high hills of the earth."

• In Psalm 139:13-14, the psalmist has this assurance: "If I take the wings of the morning, and dwell in the uttermost parts of the sea, even there Your hand shall lead me."

• Psalm 37:3-4 tells us: "Trust in the Lord, and do good; dwell in the land, and feed on His faithfulness. Delight yourself also in the Lord, and He shall give you the desires of your heart."

• In Psalm 145:15-16, the psalmist says to God, "The eyes of all look expectantly to You, and You give them their food in due season. You open Your hand and satisfy the desire of every living thing."

Being a Christian is not following a set of rules. It is following a Person, getting acquainted with Christ. It has been said, "Christ does not want us to work through Him. He wants us to let Him do His work through us, using us as a pencil to write with—or, better still, as one of the fingers of His hand." Ephesians 2:10 says, "For we are His workmanship, created in Christ Jesus for good works, which God prepared beforehand that we should walk in them."

Deuteronomy 32:6 warns those who choose the broad way over the narrow gate: "Do you thus deal with the Lord, O foolish and unwise people? Is He not your Father, who bought you? Has He not made you and established you?"

Listen again to Matthew 7:13-14 in modern translations:

• "Heaven can be entered only through the narrow gate! The highway to hell is broad, and its gate is wide enough for all the multitudes who choose its easy way. But the Gateway to Life is small, and the road is narrow, and only a few ever find it" (Living Bible).

• "Go in through the narrow gate, because the gate to hell is wide and the road that leads to it is easy, and there are many who travel it. But the gate to life is narrow and the way that leads to it is hard, and there are few people who find it" (Good News Translation).

Why Hobbies?[55]

A hobby is a favourite subject or occupation which is not one's main business.

1. Talents. As we have seen in Scripture, all have been given one or more talents. As we make use of these, we often develop other talents that we did not know we possessed. As we need bodily exercise, so we also need mental exercise, and a hobby often provides mental stimulation.

2. Learning. As we get older, we often get in a rut, but "As long as a person keeps his curiosity alive, as long as he wants to learn and tries to learn, he can continue to learn new things as long as he lives." Grandma Moses is a well-known and highly successful American folk artist who only began painting seriously at age 78.

3. Relaxation. The happiest person is one who has a balance of satisfaction. Everyone needs recreation that will be a change from work. A hobby is almost an essential in providing balance in your activities, in supplying supplementary satisfaction for your basic needs.

4. Contact with Others. A hobby can bring you into contact with others. Winter is coming with its stormy days, and human contact is even more essential then.

Doers

James 1:19-27

Let us consider the verse "Be doers of the word, and not hearers only" (James 1:22).

What are doers?

If we were to ask the leaders of almost any organization, I think they would all be glad to have a few more "doers."

---

[55] Women's Auxiliary. This meditation seems to be based on a book called *Psychology for Living.*

In this passage, we are told that if a man is a hearer of the Word and not a doer, he is "like a man observing his natural face in a mirror" who then "goes away, and immediately forgets what kind of man he was" (James 1:23-24). He sees things that should be done and then goes away and forgets all about it. Perhaps, when we go to church, we are stirred by a fine sermon and resolve that in the future our lives will be different, but unless we put it into practice immediately, we will forget about it. One of the founders of the Sick Children's Hospital in Toronto had as his motto: "I shall pass through this world but once. Any good therefore that I can do or any kindness that I can show to any human being, let me do it now; let me not defer or neglect it, for I shall not pass this way again."[56]

We are not only to be doers but doers of the Word. Martha might be called a doer, but it was Mary who won the praise of Jesus. In order to learn what a doer of the Word is, we might turn to the Bible and consider some of its commandments. Most of the Ten Commandments begin with the words, "You shall not." Many people spend all their time obeying the "shall nots," and their lives are occupied with trying to avoid anything that is sinful, so much so that they don't have time for anything else.

It is good to know the things that ought to be left out of life, but better to know the things that should be put into life. The commandments of the New Testament are positive ones, not "You shall not" but "You shall."

When Jesus was asked which were the greatest commandments, He said, "'You shall love the Lord your God with all your heart, with all your soul, and with all your mind.' This is the first and great commandment. And the second is like it: 'You shall love your neighbor as yourself.' On these two commandments hang all the Law and the Prophets" (Matthew 22:37-39). If we fill our lives with the commandments of

---

[56] The quote is originally attributed to Stephen Grellet (1772-1855), a prominent French-American Quaker missionary.

Christ, we won't have time for hate or wrongdoing. The "don'ters" might lead blameless lives, but they do not accomplish anything. Achievement belongs to the doers. It is said that John Wesley's motto was:

Do all the good you can
In all the ways you can
To all the people you can
Just as long as you can.

But before we can do, we must be. We cannot work for Christ until we have felt His power within our lives. In the parable of the vine and the branches, Jesus told His disciples, "As the branch cannot bear fruit of itself, unless it abides in the vine, neither can you, unless you abide in Me" (John 15:4) and later, "Without Me you can do nothing" (John 15:5). Paul, too, realized that he needed help. In Philippians 4:13, he said, "I can do all things through Christ who strengthens me."

One interpretation of James 1:23-24 is by an eleven-year-old named Christine Hare: "A person goes to Sunday school and hears the lesson and says, 'Hey, that's neat!' and then goes home and forgets all about it."[57]

Overflowing Power[58]
Matthew 28:16-20, Acts 1:7-8

In reading over the Great Commission, I wonder if we emphasize the command of Jesus and ignore the verse that precedes it. We notice that Jesus told His disciples, "Go therefore and make disciples of all the nations" (Matthew 28:19), but do we also see the preceding verse: "All authority has been given to Me in heaven and on earth"? In the King James Version, the Greek word for "authority" is translated as "power." In Luke 24:49, Jesus told His disciples they were to

---

[57] Christine Hare was likely a student in Mom's Sunday school class.
[58] Ladies Aid, October 1957.

wait in Jerusalem until they were given this power before attempting to start on the task He had given them.

The New Testament is full of stories of what ordinary people were able to accomplish through the power of God: "And they went out and preached everywhere, the Lord working with them and confirming the word through the accompanying signs" (Mark 16:20). Most of Jesus' disciples were unlearned men who had been called from humble tasks, and yet think of the change that took place when they received God's power at Pentecost. Peter seemed very afraid of what people might say on the night of Jesus' betrayal, yet after the resurrection he seems utterly fearless.

Are we making use of God's power to enrich our lives nowadays? We are told that Jesus Christ "is the same yesterday, today, and forever" (Hebrews 13:8). Therefore, should we not be right in assuming that God will not call us to any task without first giving us the power to accomplish it?

As we look about us, we cannot help but notice that all of God's creation has the character of being full and running over (Luke 6:38). Nearly always, nature supplies us with more than we need. Think of the surplus of fruit and vegetables we often have in our gardens and which often go to waste because we cannot use them all. Then there is the surplus of wheat in the Canadian prairies. The apostle Paul confidently told his fellow followers of Jesus: "My God shall supply all your need according to His riches in glory by Christ Jesus" (Philippians 4:19). If God is able to supply us with all the material gifts we need, is He not also able to supply us with spiritual power?

Can you imagine any woman with an electric washing machine in her home who would go on washing clothes by hand or on a washboard because she didn't know how to use it? No. When electric washing machines came into use, everyone seemed quite willing to make use of this electrical power which would make our work easier. Yet, when God offers us His spiritual power, are we as willing to accept it?

Do you remember the parable of the vine and the branches? Jesus said, "As the branch cannot bear fruit of itself, unless it abides in the vine, neither can you, unless you abide in Me. I am the vine, you are the branches. He who abides in Me, and I in him, bears much fruit; for without Me you can do nothing...If you abide in Me, and My words abide in you, you will ask what you desire, and it shall be done for you" (John 15:3-7). Therefore, if we wish to become more fruitful Christians, we have only to ask and we shall be given power to accomplish this. But, of course, it involves a risk because God always answers prayer and sometimes He answers in a very different but better way than we would expect.

In his sermon on Sunday night, Mr. Shaw was speaking of the grace of God, which he said was the power of God. One of the points he emphasized was that this power needs to be renewed daily. Just as a motor needs to be in contact with the electric current, so we must maintain our contact with God through prayer. I wonder if perhaps it isn't something like the manna in the wilderness. God gives us the amount we require as we go along. As we finish one task, we are given strength for the next. Through prayer, we not only are given power to do our own tasks, but prayer seems to be one of the best ways in which we can assist others. Would not the missionaries be severely handicapped if it were not for the prayers of the people back home? And if we were more diligent and earnest in our prayers for our missionaries, I wonder if perhaps they might be able to accomplish more than they are now doing. With the launching of the first satellite, we are beginning to catch a glimpse of what may be accomplished in the world of science. So, too, perhaps there is a vast power in prayer which needs to be explored—and that is a field in which ordinary people like us can participate.

Wings[59]

Isaiah 40:28-31, 41:10,13

One of the favourite stories at our house used to be *Mrs. Hen Goes to Market*[60]:

Henrietta Hen lay in bed and opened one eye. She knew it was morning, but she didn't want to get up. She thought, "Everyone else is going to do something wonderful today. But I shall do the same old things I do every day—cook the breakfast, wash the dishes, sweep the floor, and go to the market." But she got up and grumbled as she did each task. She finally went to the market and made some purchases and was on the way home, still grumbling that nothing ever happened to her, when it began to rain. She opened her umbrella, but at the same time a big gust of wind lifted her into the air. She was so busy trying to hang on to her parcels as well as the umbrella that she didn't notice that she was high above the ground. She dropped her purse and her parcels one by one, and she was just thinking it was fun drifting along with her umbrella when "swoosh," her umbrella blew inside out. She began to drop to earth and in her fright began to flap her wings. Then she noticed she wasn't falling anymore and realized she was flying. "Oh," she said. "This is wonderful. I shall fly all over town." And she did! She flew over the apple orchard and the cabbage patch and over the river and just missed the church steeple. "Things look different from up here," she thought. Finally, she flew home with a happy look on her face.

---

[59] Nancy Mitchell Mission Circle, November 1958.
[60] Godfrey Lynn, *Mrs. Hen Goes to Market* (Rand McNally Junior Elf Book, 1949).

The story ends by saying:

Henrietta doesn't mind getting up in the morning anymore. She jumps out of bed singing and hustles with the cooking and hustles with the dishes. She just can't wait to go to market because now Henrietta flies to market every day.

Often, as I read this story, I have felt very sympathetic toward Henrietta. I think all of us have days when we are just like Henrietta and dread facing the monotonous tasks ahead of us. But do we try her remedy?

Isaiah 40:31 says that those who wait on the Lord "shall mount up with wings like eagles." Through prayer and communion with God, we are lifted up above our daily tasks and find, like Henrietta, that "Things look different from up here"—and we go back to our ordinary tasks feeling that things are not so bad after all.

We do not think of the hen as a good flyer. Is that because it doesn't use its wings? Wings are strengthened by use, and the more we seek God through prayer and Bible reading, the stronger our wings will become.

But, even as Henrietta found that there were tasks waiting for her when she got back to earth, so, too, there are jobs awaiting us. But we find, with God's help, that we can "run and not be weary" and "walk and not faint" (Isaiah 40:31).

I was interested in seeing what the Bible had to say about wings, and I found this verse: "If I take the wings of the morning, and dwell in the uttermost parts of the sea, even there Your hand shall lead me, and Your right hand shall hold me" (Psalm 139:9-10). No matter where we go, we cannot fly beyond God's loving care.

In case we feel that our own wings shall fail, we have this promise in Psalm 91:1,4: "He who dwells in the secret place of the Most High shall abide under the shadow of the Almighty...He shall cover you with His feathers, and under His wings you shall take refuge; His truth shall be your shield and buckler."

In Isaiah 41:10,13, God promises: "Fear not, for I am with you; be not dismayed, for I am your God. I will strengthen you, yes, I will help you, I will uphold you with My righteous right hand...I, the Lord your God, will hold your right hand, saying to you, 'Fear not, I will help you.'"

On the back of the church calendar last Sunday was this verse: "Be anxious for nothing, but in everything by prayer and supplication, with thanksgiving, let your requests be made known to God; and the peace of God, which surpasses all understanding, will guard your hearts and minds through Christ Jesus" (Philippians 4:6-7).

The Desires of Our Heart[61]
Psalm 37:1-8

In Psalm 37, verse 3, we are told that if we trust in the Lord, we shall "dwell in the land" and we will "feed on His faithfulness." That is, we are told that God is able to provide for all our needs. In verse 4, we are told that if we delight in the Lord, "He shall give you the desires of your heart" (KJV). We can see where God has provided for our needs, but is it right to ask Him to satisfy all of our desires too?

Psalm 145:16 repeats the promise that God will "satisfy the desire of every living thing." God provides us with the things that will bring us lasting happiness—not the things we think we want today but might not want next week.

And yet, all around us, people are going through real trials and meeting problems for which there seems no immediate solution. Is God giving them the desires of their hearts? No one ever desires pain and suffering. Ecclesiastes 3:1-8 tell us that there is "a season, a time for every purpose under heaven." In our lives, we have winter seasons and storms. As we look back over our lives, often the things that stand out are the bad times

---

[61] Goodwill Bible Class, February 1978.

when we were challenged to put forth the extra effort or when friends gave us a helping hand. Then, we can see why things worked out as they did:

• "The Lord will perfect that which concerns me" (Psalm 138:8). That is, the Lord will work out His plans for my life.

• "Your eyes saw my substance, being yet unformed. And in Your book they all were written, the days fashioned for me, when as yet there were none of them" (Psalm 139:16). That is, God had scheduled each day of my life before I started to breathe.

• "You comprehend my path and my lying down, and are acquainted with all my ways" (Psalm 139:3). In other words, God charts the path ahead of us and tells us where to stop and rest.

• Because of all this, we should "Rest in the Lord, and wait patiently for Him" (Psalm37:7).

Our God is a God who delights in doing the impossible:

• In Genesis 18:14: God asked Abraham, "Is anything too hard for the Lord?" This was just before God miraculously gave Abraham and Sarah a son in their old age.

• In Luke 1:37, God's messenger told Mary, "With God nothing will be impossible."

• In Luke 18:27, Jesus taught, "The things which are impossible with men are possible with God."

• In Ephesians 3:20-21, Paul prayed, "Now to Him who is able to do exceedingly abundantly above all that we ask or think, according to the power that works in us, to Him be glory in the church by Christ Jesus to all generations, forever and ever."

The Encouragement of Joshua[62]

Joshua 1:1-9

Reading the newspapers and listening to radio and TV reports nowadays can sometimes be rather depressing when we hear of all the unrest in our world. We are reminded of the conversation between the Robin and the Sparrow:

Said the Robin to the Sparrow,
"I should really like to know
Why these restless human beings
Rush about and worry so."
Said the Sparrow to the Robin,
"I think that it must be
That they have no Heavenly Father
Such as cares for you and me."[63]

We often need to be reminded that if we accept Christ as our Saviour and put our trust in God, we, too, may receive the encouragement that Joshua did in Joshua 1:9: "Be strong and of good courage; do not be afraid, nor be dismayed, for the Lord your God is with you wherever you go." Perhaps, like Joshua, we are asked to do some task or we see some job that we feel should be done, but we feel that we haven't the strength or ability to do it. The other day, while searching for a subject for tonight, I came across these words in Isaiah 41:13: "For I, the Lord your God, will hold your right hand, saying to you, 'Fear not, I will help you.'"

Then I began to think of how, in the Bible stories, when God called anyone to a task, He always provided them with the strength and ability to do it and promised His help. When Moses was called by God, he did not feel that he was able to speak to the people, but God provided him with a spokesman,

---

[62] Ladies Aid, May 8, 1958.
[63] "Overheard in an Orchard," by Elizabeth Cheney, 1859.

his brother Aaron. As we read the Bible stories, we sometimes wonder why God chose such humble people to work with Him. Yet we find that when these people were willing to put their small talent into God's hands and to work in partnership with Him, they were able to overcome all obstacles. By accepting God's plan for our lives, we can make of them something far greater than we could ever work out for ourselves.

Have you ever noticed how many verses there are in the Bible in which God promises to give us strength?

• "He gives power to the weak, and to those who have no might He increases strength. Even the youths shall faint and be weary, and the young men shall utterly fall, but those who wait on the Lord shall renew their strength; they shall mount up with wings like eagles, they shall run and not be weary, they shall walk and not faint" (Isaiah 40:29-31).

• "The Lord is my light and my salvation; whom shall I fear?" (Psalm 27:1).

• "God is our refuge and strength, a very present help in trouble" (Psalm 46:1).

Perhaps if we feel we have no extra strength in ourselves, we may discover that God says to us as He did to Paul: "My grace is sufficient for you, for My strength is made perfect in weakness" (2 Corinthians 12:9). We may also learn, by accepting God's help, to say, "I can do all things through Christ who strengthens me" (Philippians 4:13). There is a verse which I am sure is familiar to all of us:

God hath not promised skies always blue,
Flower-strewn pathways all our lives through;
God hath not promised sun without rain,
Joy without sorrow, peace without pain.
But God hath promised strength for the day,
Rest for the labor, light for the way,
Grace for the trials, help from above,
Unfailing sympathy, undying love.[64]

---

[64] Annie Johnson Flint, "God Hath Not Promised."

If our lives were always sunny and peaceful, we would never feel our need of God. It is only when trials come to us that we really learn what it is to depend on Him and to find out that nothing is able to separate us from the love of Christ (Romans 8:38-39).

Today it seems that whenever we listen to TV or radio announcements, we are always being offered a bonus. By buying a certain kind of soap or cereal we can get an extra gift or premium. The Bible is never out of date, and it offers us the greatest premium of all. We are told that God is "able to do exceedingly abundantly above all that we ask or think" (Ephesians 3:20). And so, not only does God give us strength and courage to help us day by day, but the gift of peace as well. Jesus says in John 14:27, "Peace I leave with you, My peace I give to you." Besides peace, we may also receive the added gift of joy. Isaiah 12:2 says, "I will trust and not be afraid; 'For Yah, the Lord, is my strength and song." If songs fill our hearts, there is no room for fear.

Therefore, let us take the advice of King George VI in his Christmas message of 1939: "Go out into the darkness and put your hand into the Hand of God. That shall be to you better than light and safer than a known way."[65]

Impossibles[66]

Mark 9:14-29

In the story told in this passage, the disciple had tried to heal a boy possessed by an evil spirit but had failed. Yet, just three chapters earlier, in Mark 6:7-13 the disciples had been sent out two by two and had been given power over unclean spirits, and they had "cast out many demons."

---

[65] Minnie Louise Haskins, "God Knows" (also known as "The Gate of the Year"), 1908.
[66] Afternoon Mission Circle, February 20, 1963.

Are we like the disciples? Sometimes we pray and feel our prayers are answered, but once in a while we come up against something too big for us. We pray about it but just don't seem to get anywhere with our prayers. In a case like this, do we take the problem to Jesus and ask Him what the trouble is (Mark 9:28)?

The *Sunday School Times* carried an article called "What is the Trouble?" It pointed out that in giving the disciples the answer that "This kind can come out by nothing but prayer and fasting" (Mark 9:29), Jesus was admitting that some problems are tougher than others. Each one is different, and some need a special solution. The writer explained, "Band aids are wonderful but are no good for cancer." Here, Jesus seemed to be telling the disciples that this was a difficult case. The writer imagined that he was with the disciples, and when Jesus said, "This kind can come out by nothing..." they would interrupt Him and say, "You are certainly right. This is a really tough case. We can cure some cases, but this is impossible." Then the writer imagines that Jesus repeated the sentence again and this time was allowed to finish: "This kind can come out by nothing but prayer and fasting."

Do we sometimes write "impossible" over certain situations? We forget what Jesus told the father of the sick boy: "If you can believe, all things are possible to him who believes" (Mark 9:23). A Sunday school superintendent in Scotland invited a boy, who was a juvenile delinquent, to Sunday school. Three times. The superintendent even bought him a suit. Finally, the boy was converted. He was Robert Morrison, who became the first missionary to China. The superintendent might have thought this juvenile delinquent was an impossible case, but he wasn't.

Jesus said that some difficult situations require fasting. Fasting is the voluntary letting go of something that is legitimately mine for the sake of a higher goal. Sometimes we have to choose between what is good and what is best.

Here are some other biblical passages on "impossibles":

• When Mary thought it was impossible for her to give birth to the Messiah since she was a virgin, God's angel told her, "With God nothing will be impossible" (Luke 1:37).

• When Jesus said, "It is easier for a camel to go through the eye of a needle than for a rich man to enter the kingdom of God," those who heard Him said, "Who then can be saved?" Jesus answered, "The things which are impossible with men are possible with God" (Luke 18:25-27).

• Hebrews 11:6 teaches us: "Without faith it is impossible to please Him, for he who comes to God must believe that He is, and that He is a rewarder of those who diligently seek Him."

So, too, it is with missions. There are so few workers, and it is such a big task (Matthew 9:36-38). Workers have never been plentiful. But Jesus told us to pray that there will be workers. With God, the impossible becomes possible.

Living Our Mission[67]
Colossians 3:12-17

This year, our theme is "Living Our Mission." The subject scares me a little. It is easier to talk about than to put into practice.

But, as I look back on the past forty years, I realize just how many lessons on how to live I have learned from the mission circle.

When I was growing up, we took it for granted that Canada was a Christian country. The schools and churches worked together. In rural districts, there were very few who didn't attend church, and almost no one worked on Sunday. But now, times have changed, and we begin to realize that unless we more actively live our mission, Christians will become an endangered species. As one drives along the 401 Highway and

---

[67] Hagersville, 1987. This was at a joint meeting of several mission circles.

sees all the new subdivisions going up in the Toronto area, one wonders how the gospel will ever reach the people moving there.

Jesus told His followers they were to be His witnesses first in their hometown of Jerusalem, then in Judea and Samaria and to the ends of the earth (Acts 1:8). The prospect of witnessing in one's home and hometown is frightening. But Jesus told His disciples that first they would receive the power of the Holy Spirit and the witnessing would follow.

I have attended sessions on how to witness, and we were given a formula, but when I tried to follow through, I was always a failure.

Then, at the mission circle convention in Waterloo, I attended a seminar conducted by Joan Wilton on "Witnessing—Naturally!" Her advice was to "Mind your manners and be yourself." Each person is different, and she suggested witnessing could be accomplished by such acts as inviting a neighbour in for a cup of coffee or tea—which made it seem simple. She told how she was able to pass on her faith as an emergency room nurse. She also emphasized the importance of letting people feel they are loved, and I have realized what a difference that makes when teaching Sunday school. Now I begin to wonder if it is possible for people to realize God's love for them if they have never experienced human love. Colossians 3:14 (NIV) reminds us: "Over all these virtues put on love, which binds them all together in perfect unity."

At one of our mission circle workshops when Mary Hansen was director of our association, she suggested that we use this prayer: "Lord, what do You want me to do for You today?" I am beginning to learn that when God arranges our schedule, we can accomplish so much more (and His service also provides a wonderful benefit package).

Then, this month while reading the October *Canadian Baptist*, I came across an update for the prayer, "Lord, what do You want me to do for You today?" The suggestion is that it be revised to: "Lord, what do You want to do through me?" That makes all the difference in the world, because then He is providing the power to help us really live our mission.

Prayer: Our Heavenly Father, thank You for our association and the chance to meet with other circles. We thank You for all the faithful workers of our association who through the years have lived their faith and given us an example. We pray for this meeting this afternoon and for those who will take part. Please give them the message You want us to hear, that we will be inspired and given power to pass on Your love to others. We pray for the executive of the association that You will guide and direct them and give them strength for their task. We think of so many of our members who are older and no longer able to get out to meetings as they once did. We ask that You will be with and comfort them and that workers may be found to carry on the task of proclaiming the message of salvation. Amen.

A Broken Wrist[68]

Recently, I broke my wrist. It was painful and inconvenient. I found these verses helpful in dealing with this:
• "I will certainly be with you" (Exodus 3:12).
• "I will never leave you nor forsake you" (Hebrews 13:5).
• "My grace is sufficient for you, for My strength is made perfect in weakness" (2 Corinthians 12:9).
• "Trust in the Lord forever, for in Yah, the Lord, is everlasting strength" (Isaiah 26:4).
• "In returning and rest you shall be saved; in quietness and confidence shall be your strength" (Isaiah 30:15).
• "Your ears shall hear a word behind you, saying, 'This is the way, walk in it,' whenever you turn to the right hand or whenever you turn to the left" (Isaiah 30:21).

---

[68] October 1974.

- "Those who wait on the Lord shall renew their strength" (Isaiah 40:31).

These verses are helpful for any time we are dealing with problems and weaknesses.

Pioneers[69]
Hebrews 11:1-10, 12:1-2

On Sunday, we will celebrate our church anniversary, a day when we think of the pioneers who first settled in this country and who laboured to establish a church for themselves and those who would follow them. We are thankful that they built such a fine church, one that we can still be proud of even today. The pioneers must have been people of great faith and courage to move to a new country and build new homes, schools, and churches there. They remind us of the verses we read about Abraham.

The Winston Dictionary defines "pioneer" as "one who goes before to prepare the way for others."

I received some information about pioneer life at Thanksgiving while spending the weekend in New Liskeard.[70] I attended an evening service in which the senior citizens of that community were the special guests. During the time of fellowship afterwards, everyone was asked to stand and tell how long they had been in the north and where they had come from. New Liskeard is on the edge of the Great Clay Belt, and the land was first opened up about sixty years ago. Almost everyone there had come from southern Ontario (including one person from Caledonia, near here). Many had come to New Liskeard before the railroad was built and had travelled by boat up the Ottawa River and Lake Temiskaming. Church

---

[69] October 20, 1960.

[70] Mom's half-brother, James Young, was a United Church minister in this town in northern Ontario.

services were held in schoolhouses until churches were established. Some people had lost everything in the big forest fire in the early 1920s, and all seemed to have endured many hardships, although, looking back, they seemed to consider it to have been more of an adventure.

I wonder if the people who built our church realized how much they were doing for those who would come after them. We are dependent today on so many other people and also on the work and knowledge of the pioneers who have gone before to prepare the way for us. Each new discovery is the result of someone working with the knowledge gained by others.

In the radio program *Lift Up Your Hearts*, a man told of moving to a new house in the wintertime. When spring came, he was delighted by the number of spring bulbs that blossomed. He had not planted them and did not even know they were there. The former owner, in beautifying the place for his own pleasure, also gave it to those who lived in the house after him. Any worthwhile thing we do for ourselves also benefits others.

In one sense, are we not also pioneers, going ahead to prepare the way for our children and those who will follow after us?

Our actions and the kind of lives we lead will perhaps determine what kind of church and what kind of town we will have fifty or a hundred years from now. It is said that the greatest advertisement of a garden is the flowers it produces, and the greatest advertisement of Christianity is in the Christian lives it develops. People might not come to church, but they can watch us.

Finally, let us consider the phrase "looking unto Jesus, the author and finisher of our faith" (Hebrews 12:2). In the Revised Standard Version, this reads, "looking to Jesus the pioneer and perfecter of our faith." In our Christian living, we are not stepping out into unexplored territory, but we know that Christ, the Great Pioneer, has gone before, leaving us a guidebook (the Bible). He also told us that He would go to prepare a place for us. May we ever be willing to follow in His footsteps, that others, watching us, may see Christ in us and want to follow Him too.

Earthen Vessels[71]

At this season of the year, we are reminded of God's goodness to us as we look at the trees in their autumn colours. On Sunday, we were reminded of the variety of fruits and vegetables He has provided for our enjoyment.[72] I am sure that as we see the pictures later, we will be reminded of God's greatness in creating things like mountains and lakes.

But sometimes earth brings us many problems, and we have many questions for which we can't find answers. For instance, why do these bodies of ours have a habit of letting us down just when we think we have so much planned? Or perhaps life hasn't turned out just as we had expected, and we wonder why.

2 Corinthians 4:6-7 says: "For it is the God who commanded light to shine out of darkness, who has shone in our hearts to give the light of the knowledge of the glory of God in the face of Jesus Christ. But we have this treasure in earthen vessels, that the excellence of the power may be of God and not of us." (God's packaging is very different from ours. No matter how poor or inappropriate the gifts we give, we wrap them in shiny paper and ribbons. For God, it is what is inside that matters.)

As we study the Bible, we find many instances where people are spoken of as earthenware jars or vessels. Everyone I am sure is familiar with Jeremiah 18:1-6, where God told Jeremiah to go and watch a potter making clay pots and God

---

[71] Goodwill Bible Class, 1975.
[72] On Thanksgiving Sunday, the sanctuary of Waterford Baptist Church was usually decorated with locally grown produce and flowers.

said: "O house of Israel, can I not do with you as this potter? Look, as the clay is in the potter's hand, so are you in My hand, O house of Israel!" This idea is repeated in Isaiah 45:9-12, which says that we have no more right to question how our Creator made us than a clay pot has to question its maker: "Shall the clay say to him who forms it, 'What are you making?'" Psalm 115:3 says, "But our God is in heaven; He does whatever He pleases."

As we read the passage in Isaiah, we are reminded that God made us in a certain form and for a certain purpose and we haven't any right to argue with Him about it. Mr. Wilton[73] a few Sundays ago spoke of everything serving God's plan. The New Testament, too, reminds us that we are formed according to God's plans, and in Romans there is a passage very similar to that in Isaiah. Do you remember that verse? "Does not the potter have power over the clay, from the same lump to make one vessel for honor and another for dishonor?" (Romans 9:21). Phillips translation says: "The potter, for instance, is always assumed to have complete control over the clay, making with one part of the lump a lovely vase, and with another a pipe for sewage." But I like best the way the Living Bible expresses it: "Who are you to criticize God? Should the thing made say to the one who made it, 'Why have you made me like this?' When a man makes a jar out of clay, doesn't he have a right to use the same lump of clay to make one jar beautiful, to be used for holding flowers, and another to throw garbage into? Does not God have a perfect right to show his fury and power against those who are fit only for destruction, those he has been patient with for all this time? And he has a right to take others such as ourselves, who have been made for pouring the riches of his glory into, whether we are Jews or Gentiles, and to be kind to us so that everyone can see how very great his glory is" (Romans 9:20-23).

---

[73] Lyle and Mary Wilton were missionaries who were for a time members of Waterford Baptist Church.

My Sunday school class last year were very interested in this verse, to think that some people were like beautiful vases and others like garbage cans. ("Hey, that's neat!") And don't despise the garbage cans. I have learned the last few years just how valuable they can be. The Weymouth New Testament[74] says, "We have this treasure in a fragile vase of clay that the exceeding greatness of the power may be seen to be of God and not originate in us."

A fragile vase of clay.
Well, this being so, I pray
That it not be too hard for God to press
It into comeliness
And not too thick
For Him to glimmer through it pure and quick.
Because if through such clay
He will consent to shine,
The glory must be His,
The gladness mine.

Thanksgiving[75]

Next Monday, we will celebrate Thanksgiving—a day set aside for thanking God for all His goodness to us. As we sit down to Thanksgiving dinner, may we not only be thankful for all we have to eat, but may we also remember with thankfulness all the people who have worked together so that we might enjoy it—not only the farmers and storekeepers in our own country, but also people in faraway lands who produce the coffee, tea, and spices which add variety to our meals. As we consider this, we realize our dependence on

---

[74] The Weymouth New Testament (WNT), also known as *The New Testament in Modern Speech* or *The Modern Speech New Testament,* is in the public domain.
[75] Ladies Aid, October 8, 1959.

others and how many different people have worked so that we might enjoy our Thanksgiving dinner.

Let us not only be thankful to others who have helped us but also remember God and His part in making things grow. We may select the best seed and prepare the soil in the best way, but unless God sends His rain and sunshine, our efforts will be in vain. Yet we remember the promise of God to Noah in Genesis 8:22: "While the earth remains, seedtime and harvest, cold and heat, winter and summer, and day and night shall not cease."

At this Thanksgiving time, are there not other things for which we might be thankful? As I thought on this, I wondered what the Bible has to say on Thanksgiving. I looked up the verses on thanks and thanksgiving listed in the Concordance and was amazed at how many verses there were on the subject in the writings of Paul. Paul was a man who worked very hard in his missionary work and who suffered many afflictions in spreading the gospel, and yet his letters seem to be filled with rejoicing. Let us try to find out why Paul was thankful.

One of Paul's main causes for thanksgiving was that God had sent His Son Jesus Christ to be his Saviour and the Saviour of all those who will believe in Him:
• "Thanks be to God for His indescribable gift!" (2 Corinthians 9:15)
• "Thanks be to God, who gives us the victory through our Lord Jesus Christ" (1 Corinthians 15:57).

Then Paul thanked God for his friends and for their faith:
• "I thank my God through Jesus Christ for you all, that your faith is spoken of throughout the whole world" (Romans 1:8).
• "I also, after I heard of your faith in the Lord Jesus and your love for all the saints, do not cease to give thanks for you, making mention of you in my prayers" (Ephesians 1:15-16).

Another thing I noticed about Paul's thankfulness to God was that he was always thankful—not just when things were going smoothly or at Thanksgiving time. When Paul and Silas were put in prison, we are told that "at midnight Paul and Silas were praying and singing hymns to God" (Acts 16:25).

Besides being thankful always, Paul exhorted the followers of Christ to be thankful in all things:
• "Rejoice always, pray without ceasing, in everything give thanks" (1 Thessalonians 5:16-18).
• "By Him let us continually offer the sacrifice of praise to God" (Hebrews 13:15).
• "Be filled with the Spirit, speaking to one another in psalms and hymns and spiritual songs, singing and making melody in your heart to the Lord, giving thanks always for all things to God the Father in the name of our Lord Jesus Christ" (Ephesians 5:18-20).

Let us follow Paul's recipe for a happy Thanksgiving.

Thanksgiving 2[76]

At Thanksgiving, we are especially reminded of God's goodness to us. Our church is decorated with fruits and vegetables. The Norfolk County Fall Fair has large displays of fruits and vegetables. In our families, we celebrate with bountiful Thanksgiving dinners.

In Genesis 8:22, God promised: "While the earth remains, seedtime and harvest, cold and heat, winter and summer, and day and night shall not cease."

In Deuteronomy 8:7-18, God told the Israelites: "For the Lord your God is bringing you into a good land, a land of brooks of water, of fountains and springs, that flow out of valleys and hills; a land of wheat and barley, of vines and fig trees and pomegranates, a land of olive oil and honey; a land in which you will eat bread without scarcity, in which you will lack nothing..." But then God warned: "When you have eaten and are full, then you shall bless the Lord your God for the good

---

[76] Mission Circle, October 7, 1981.

land which He has given you. Beware that you do not forget the Lord your God by not keeping His commandments...lest—when you have eaten and are full, and have built beautiful houses and dwell in them; and when your herds and your flocks multiply, and your silver and your gold are multiplied, and all that you have is multiplied...—then you say in your heart, 'My power and the might of my hand have gained me this wealth.'" The passage ends with this solemn warning: "Remember the Lord your God, for it is He who gives you power to get wealth."

In Luke 12:48, Jesus warned, "Everyone to whom much is given, from him much will be required." As we see pictures of famine in Africa, we realize how much we have. Then, too, there is a scarcity of Bibles in some parts of the world. We have much to be thankful for, but that means we also have much to be responsible for.

But what about those among us who have troubles? At this Thanksgiving season, the Bible also has words for those of us encountering difficulties:

• Ephesians 5:20 encourages us to be filled with God's Spirit, "giving thanks always for all things to God the Father in the name of our Lord Jesus Christ." Note that it says to give thanks *always* for *all* things.

• Job rightly asked: "Shall we indeed accept good from God, and shall we not accept adversity?" (Job 2:10).

• Job struggled to know where God was in the midst of his troubles: "Oh, that I knew where I might find Him...I go forward, but He is not there, and backward, but I cannot perceive Him" (Job 23:3,8). But then, in faith, Job affirmed: "But He knows the way that I take; when He has tested me, I shall come forth as gold" (Job 23:10).

• The apostle Paul reminded us that "The things which are seen are temporary, but the things which are not seen are eternal" (2 Corinthains 4:18). Our troubles are temporary, but the more important things last forever.

What are some of these eternal things for which we should be thankful?

1. God's Faithfulness

Do we ever thank God for:

• The fact that we can approach Him at any time?

• The fact that He is eternal and never changes and always keeps His promises?

2. God's Provision

Do we have a proper appreciation for the way in which things work out when our lives are committed to Him? Aren't you glad that we only have one day at a time to worry about?

3. God's Personal Love for Us

Do we ever thank God that we are each known to Him by name? To the government, we have a social insurance number. The telephone company gives us a phone number. Credit card companies give us a credit card number. That is not how God knows us:

• "He calls his own sheep by name and leads them out" (John 10:3).

• "Rejoice because your names are written in heaven" (Luke 10:20).

• Revelation reminds us that our names are written in "the Lamb's Book of Life" (Revelation 3:5, 21:27).

It is Thanksgiving, and we have much to be thankful for. "Therefore by Him let us continually offer the sacrifice of praise to God, that is, the fruit of our lips, giving thanks to His name" (Hebrews 13:15).

Stars[77]

Psalm 8:3-9, Matthew 10:29-31

Did you ever stop to think how often stars are mentioned in the Bible? We are told in the first chapter of Genesis: "Then

---

[77] Ladies Aid, May 12, 1960.

God made two great lights: the greater light to rule the day, and the lesser light to rule the night. He made the stars also" (Genesis 1:16).

In Genesis 15:5, Abraham was told to "Look now toward heaven, and count the stars if you are able to number them…So shall your descendants be."

David, too, seemed to be one who looked at the stars and managed to catch a glimpse of the glory and majesty of God: "The heavens declare the glory of God; and the firmament shows His handiwork" (Psalm 19:1).

Isaiah, too, had the ability to look at the stars and realize the greatness of God: "Thus says the Lord: 'Heaven is My throne, and earth is My footstool'" (Isaiah 66:1). The 40th chapter of Isaiah also tells of God's omnipotence. Isaiah 40:12 declares that God "has measured the waters in the hollow of His hand, measured heaven with a span and calculated the dust of the earth in a measure, weighed the mountains in scales and the hills in a balance." Isaiah 40:26 says: "Lift up your eyes on high, and see who has created these things, who brings out their host by number; He calls them all by name, by the greatness of His might and the strength of His power; not one is missing."

When God sent His Son to earth, it was a star that led the wise men to Bethlehem to find the newborn King (Matthew 2:1-2).

In her book *Riches of the Kingdom*,[78] Grace Noll Crowell writes: "In all the universe of visible things, there is nothing that has the power to calm the spirit and rest the mind as does a long look skyward on a starlit night. A strange, surprising awareness fills the heart as one by one the silver lights appear, each to become the amazing wonder of a star. Stars are so silent, they are so unfailing, so pure and white, so steeped in peace, that the restless soul of man is stilled by their serenity.

---

[78] Grace Noll Crowell (1877-1969), *Riches of the Kingdom: Devotions for Women* (New York: Abingdon Press, 1954).

There is a comfort in them to treasure to one's innermost being."

Now that we are surrounded by so many electric lights at night, I wonder if we take the time to look up at the heavens on a starlit night.

Now that people are beginning to explore the possibilities of space travel, our attention is being drawn more and more to the stars, and yet the more we find out about our solar system and the other planets in it, the more we realize that our earth is only a very small part of a universe too great for our imaginations to comprehend.

An astronomer from Princeton University in the United States was once giving a lecture on the Milky Way. At the conclusion, a woman asked him, "If our world is so great, can we believe that God pays any attention to us?" "That, madam," the astronomer replied, "depends entirely on how big a God you believe in."

As we read our Bibles, we are repeatedly told that our God, who is great enough to call all the stars by name and to keep them in their courses, is also great enough to care for each one of us. In the same chapter where he tells of the greatness of God, Isaiah tells of His care for us: "Have you not known? Have you not heard? The everlasting God, the Lord, the Creator of the ends of the earth, neither faints nor is weary. His understanding is unsearchable. He gives power to the weak, and to those who have no might He increases strength" (Isaiah 40:18-29).

David, too, realized God's care for him: "The angel of the Lord encamps all around those who fear Him, and delivers them" (Psalm 34:7); "God is our refuge and strength, a very present help in trouble" (Psalm 46:1).

Jesus emphasized God's care for each one of us: "Are not two sparrows sold for a copper coin? And not one of them falls to the ground apart from your Father's will. But the very hairs of your head are all numbered. Do not fear therefore; you are of more value than many sparrows" (Matthew 10:29-31); "Do not worry about your life, what you will eat or what you will drink; nor about your body, what you will put on...Look at the birds of the air, for they neither sow nor reap nor gather into barns; yet your heavenly Father feeds them...Consider the lilies of the field, how they grow: they neither toil nor spin; and yet I say to you that even Solomon in all his glory was not arrayed like one of these. Now if God so clothes the grass of the field, which today is, and tomorrow is thrown into the oven, will He not much more clothe you, O you of little faith? Therefore do not worry, saying, 'What shall we eat?' or 'What shall we drink?' or 'What shall we wear?'...For your heavenly Father knows that you need all these things" (Matthew 6:25-32).

Peter, too, was sure of God's care for him, telling Christians to humbly submit themselves to God, "casting all your care upon Him, for He cares for you" (1 Peter 5:7).

It is wonderful to think that we have a God who is great enough to control the whole universe but yet at the same time cares about each one of us and is concerned about all that we do.

I know a strange and marvellous thing: I am aware
That I, a speck in the universe, am in God's care,
Am guided as safely as the stars, or the moon, or the blazing
*   sun,*
And that He is watching over me in this race I run.
Life is my orbit, and I swing out through time and space,
Held by the reins of a mighty power within my place.
Held by the hand of God Himself, I am a part of His plan
That reaches out through eternity and back, since time
*   began.*
I am aware of a marvellous thing: I am aware,
Humbly, that He considers me worthy of His care.[79]

[79] The source of this poem is unknown. The poem's author might have been Margaret Small. She was a woman confined to Toronto's Hospital for Incurables (later renamed Queen Elizabeth Hospital) who wrote pieces for the paper. Mom visited her regularly when Mom worked at the Parliament

Everlasting⁸⁰

Have you done any purchasing lately? Most new products nowadays have a warranty for only one year. If the product is defective, it is not repaired. You just mail it back to the company. People buy antiques and pay a lot of money for them. They are considered valuable because they are so rare. In our world, nothing seems to last, nothing is permanent. Is there anything that we can count on to still be here tomorrow?

God's promises are not for a few months or years but forever and ever:

• "For unto us a Child is born, unto us a Son is given; and the government will be upon His shoulder. And His name will be called Wonderful, Counselor, Mighty God, **Everlasting Father**, Prince of Peace. Of the increase of His government and peace there will be **no end**, upon the throne of David and over His kingdom, to order it and establish it with judgment and justice from that time forward, even **forever**" (Isaiah 9:6-7).

• "Then Abraham planted a tamarisk tree in Beersheba, and there called on the name of the Lord, the **Everlasting God**" (Genesis 21:33).

• "But the Lord is the true God; He is the living God and the **everlasting King**" (Jeremiah 10:10).

• "The **eternal God** is your refuge, and underneath are the **everlasting arms**" (Deuteronomy 33:27).

• "The sun shall no longer be your light by day, nor for brightness shall the moon give light to you; but the Lord will be to you an **everlasting light**, and your God your glory" (Isaiah 60:19).

• "Have you not known? Have you not heard? The **everlasting God**, the Lord, the Creator of the ends of the earth, neither faints nor is weary" (Isaiah 40:28).

Buildings in Toronto. Margaret was a devout Christian, gave Mom many poems, and had a strong influence on Mom.
⁸⁰ Goodwill Bible Class, March 21, 1984.

- "From **everlasting to everlasting**, You are God" (Psalm 90:1-2).
- "The mercy of the Lord is **from everlasting to everlasting**" (Psalm 103:17).
- "For the Lord is good; His mercy is **everlasting**, and His truth **endures to all generations**" (Psalm 100:5).
- "Keep this commandment without spot, blameless until our Lord Jesus Christ's appearing, which He will manifest in His own time, He who is the blessed and only Potentate, the King of kings and Lord of lords, who alone has **immortality**, dwelling in unapproachable light, whom no man has seen or can see, to whom be honor and **everlasting power**" (1 Timothy 6:14-16).
- "But Israel shall be saved by the Lord with an **everlasting salvation**; you shall not be ashamed or disgraced **forever and ever**" (Isaiah 45:17).
- "The Lord has appeared of old to me, saying: 'Yes, I have loved you with an **everlasting love**; therefore with lovingkindness I have drawn you'" (Jeremiah 31:3).
- "Then I saw another angel flying in the midst of heaven, having the **everlasting gospel** to preach to those who dwell on the earth—to every nation, tribe, tongue, and people" (Revelation 14:6).
- "Search me, O God, and know my heart; try me, and know my anxieties; and see if there is any wicked way in me, and lead me in **the way everlasting**" (Psalm 139:23-24).
- "Trust in the Lord **forever**, for in Yah, the Lord, is **everlasting strength**" (Isaiah 26:4).
- "For God so loved the world that He gave His only begotten Son, that whoever believes in Him should not perish but have **everlasting life**" (John 3:16).
- "Most assuredly, I say to you, he who believes in Me has **everlasting life**" (John 6:47).
- "There shall be no night there: They need no lamp nor light of the sun, for the Lord God gives them light. And they shall reign **forever and ever**" (Revelation 22:5).

A Spiritual Prayer

Psalm 119:33-40

We often pray for the things we need—money, healing, etc. But in Psalm 119:33-40, the psalmist prays that he will become more righteous and godly:

• "Teach me, O Lord, the way of Your statutes" ("and I shall keep it") (verse 33)

• "Give me understanding" ("and I shall keep Your law") (verse 34).

• "Make me walk in the path of Your commandments" (verse 35).

• "Incline my heart to Your testimonies" (verse 36).

• "Turn away my eyes from looking at worthless things" (verse 37).

• "Revive me in Your way" (verse 37).

• "Establish Your word to Your servant" (verse 38).

• "Turn away my reproach" (verse 39)

• "Revive me in Your righteousness" (verse 40).

All this comes first. Then we will be able to follow Jesus' call to be His followers:

• "Follow Me, and I will make you fishers of men" (Matthew 4:19).

• "You shall receive power when the Holy Spirit has come upon you; and you shall be witnesses to Me in Jerusalem, and in all Judea and Samaria, and to the end of the earth" (Acts 1:8).

God Keeps His Promises[81]

Numbers 14, Joshua 14:6-13, 21:45, 23:14

In Numbers 13, Moses sent twelve spies into the Promised Land. They reported that it was a good land but that the people

---

[81] Goodwill Bible Class, March 1977.

there were too powerful to overcome. Of the twelve spies, only Caleb urged the people to enter the land. In Numbers 14, because the Israelites lacked faith, God said that none of that generation would enter the Promised Land, except for Caleb. This was repeated in Numbers 32:11-12, where it was specified that no one over the age of twenty would enter the land, except for Caleb. Caleb was then forty. The Israelites then wandered in the wilderness for another forty years (Numbers 32:13).

Joshua led the next generation of Israelites into the Promised Land, and Joshua 21:45 declared: "Not a word failed of any good thing which the Lord had spoken to the house of Israel. All came to pass." Joshua himself repeated this declaration to the Israelites in Joshua 23:14. These promises included the one made to Caleb. In Joshua 14:10, Caleb said, "Behold, the Lord has kept me alive, as He said, these forty-five years"—and then Caleb received his portion of the land that he had helped to conquer. Caleb waited forty-five years for God's answer.

God keeps His promises because:

1. He never makes mistakes and never has to change His mind.

2. He is all-powerful, and so we can rely on His promises.

Hebrews 4:5 states that the previous generation of Israelites "did not enter because of disobedience" (the King James Version says they "entered not in because of unbelief"). Hebrews 11:1,6 explain: "Now faith is the substance of things hoped for, the evidence of things not seen...Without faith it is impossible to please Him, for he who comes to God must believe that He is, and that He is a rewarder of those who diligently seek Him."

These are the lessons we can learn from Caleb:

1. Caleb believed God. Faith is believing that God can "do exceedingly abundantly above all that we ask or think" (Ephesians 3:20).

2. Caleb had "a different spirit in him" (Numbers 14:24). This should also be true of us: "Therefore, if anyone is in Christ, he is a new creation; (2 Corinthians 5:17); "If anyone does not have the Spirit of Christ, he is not His" (Romans 8:9).

3. Caleb "wholly followed the Lord" (Joshua 14:8,9,14). If you believe God, it will be revealed sooner or later in how you live.

Times, Needs, and Desires[82]

On May 10, 1973, Ernie and I began questioning whether it would be possible for us to go to England. The answer did not come until September 1977, when we were finally able to make the trip. 2 Peter 3:9 assures us: "The Lord is not slack concerning His promise." The poet tells us:

He hides Himself so wondrously,
As though there were no God...
And seems to leave us to ourselves
Just when we need him most...
Thrice blest is he to whom is given
The instinct that can tell
That God is on the field
When he is most invisible.[83]

God is working for our good even when we are not aware of it. There are many Scripture verses that tell us that God works things out in His own time:

• "My times are in Your hand" (Psalm 31:15).

• "The Lord is good to those who wait for Him" (Lamentations 3:25).

• "Call to Me, and I will answer you, and show you great and mighty things, which you do not know" (Jeremiah 33:3).

---

[82] Goodwill Bible Class, February 15, 1978.
[83] Frederick W. Faber, "The Right Must Win," 1849.

• God cares about both our needs and our desires: "Trust in the Lord, and do good; dwell in the land, and feed on His faithfulness" (needs, Psalm 37:3); "Delight yourself also in the Lord, and He shall give you the desires of your heart" (desires, Psalm 37:4); "The eyes of all look expectantly to You, and You give them their food in due season (needs, Psalm 145:15); "You open Your hand and satisfy the desire of every living thing" (desires, Psalm 145:16).

• While we are waiting on God, what is our part? "This should be your ambition: to live a quiet life, minding your own business and doing your own work" (1 Thessalonians 4:11, TLB); "Study to be quiet, and to do your own business, and to work with your own hands" (1 Thessalonians 4:11, KJV).

• "Your eyes saw my substance, being yet unformed. And in Your book they all were written, the days fashioned for me, when as yet there were none of them" (Psalm 139:16).

• "The Lord will perfect that which concerns me" (Psalm 138:8). That is, the Lord will work out His plans for my life.

• "You comprehend my path and my lying down, and are acquainted with all my ways" (Psalm 139:3). That is, God charts the path ahead of me and tells me where to stop and rest.

What Does God Require?[84]

God reminds us of His greatness and His power, which He offers to use for our benefit:

• "Look to Me, and be saved, all you ends of the earth! For I am God, and there is no other" (Isaiah 45:22).

• "Call to Me, and I will answer you, and show you great and mighty things, which you do not know" (Jeremiah 33:3).

---

[84] Written January 28, 1974, delivered to Goodwill Bible Class, March 1975.

• "I will give you the treasures of darkness and hidden riches of secret places, that you may know that I, the Lord, who call you by your name, am the God of Israel" (Isaiah 45:3).

• "The Lord has anointed Me to preach good tidings to the poor; He has sent Me to heal the brokenhearted, to proclaim liberty to the captives, and the opening of the prison to those who are bound; to proclaim the acceptable year of the Lord...to comfort all who mourn, to console those who mourn in Zion, to give them beauty for ashes, the oil of joy for mourning, the garment of praise for the spirit of heaviness" (Isaiah 61:1-3).

These are precious promises. But what does God require in return?

• "For everyone to whom much is given, from him much will be required" (Luke 12:48).

• "What does the Lord your God require of you, but to fear the Lord your God, to walk in all His ways and to love Him, to serve the Lord your God with all your heart and with all your soul, and to keep the commandments of the Lord and His statutes which I command you today for your good?" (Deuteronomy 10:12-13).

• "He has shown you, O man, what is good; and what does the Lord require of you but to do justly, to love mercy, and to walk humbly with your God?" (Micah 6:8).

• "Pure and undefiled religion before God and the Father is this: to visit orphans and widows in their trouble, and to keep oneself unspotted from the world" (James 1:27).

• "It is required in stewards that one be found faithful" (1 Corinthians 4:2).

For our service, God offers a reward: "Be faithful until death, and I will give you the crown of life" (Revelation 2:10).

Troubles![85]
Psalm 34

We all face many problems. In Psalm 34, David repeatedly spoke of troubles and of God's deliverance from them all:
• "I sought the Lord, and He heard me, and delivered me from all my fears" (Psalm 34:4).
• "This poor man cried out, and the Lord heard him, and saved him out of all his troubles" (Psalm 34:6).
• "The righteous cry out, and the Lord hears, and delivers them out of all their troubles" (Psalm 34:17).
• "Many are the afflictions of the righteous, but the Lord delivers him out of them all" (Psalm 34:19).

But what if we are still in the midst of troubles and God has not yet delivered us? In Psalm 37, David tells us what to do in the meantime: "Delight yourself...in the Lord...Commit your way to the Lord, trust also in Him...Rest in the Lord, and wait patiently for Him" (Psalm 37:4,5,7). In Matthew 7:7, Jesus taught: "Ask, and it will be given to you; seek, and you will find; knock, and it will be opened to you." As well, since God has promised to deliver us from our fears, we should trust Him and not be afraid: "For God has not given us a spirit of fear, but of power and of love and of a sound mind" (1 Timothy 1:7).

In Psalm 34, God promised to deliver us from all of our fears, all of our troubles, and all of our afflictions. When do we praise God for this? After our deliverance or before? Psalm 34:1 says: "I will bless the Lord at all times." We should praise Him before He has delivered us and not just afterward.

---

[85] May 25, 1973.

The Power of God[86]

In Genesis 18, when God told Abraham and Sarah that they would have a son, they had trouble believing it since they were old. God responded: "Is anything too hard for the Lord?" (Genesis 18:14). A year later, Isaac was born.

In Ezekiel 37:1-14, God showed Ezekiel a vision of a valley full of dead bones, and God asked, "Can these bones live?" (Ezekiel 3:3). Ezekiel did not know what to say, so he said, "O Lord God, You know." God told Ezekiel to prophesy to the bones. When he did, the bones developed sinews, flesh, and skin. God commanded again, and breath came into the bodies, and they came alive again. The people of Israel were then in exile and their nation seemed as dead as the dry bones. They said, "Our hope is lost" (Ezekiel 3:11). But God told Ezekiel to tell the people that He would bring their nation back to life as he did with the bones. After seventy years, the nation was restored, and the city was eventually rebuilt.

When Jerusalem was surrounded by the Babylonian army and about to be destroyed, Jeremiah acknowledged that the city deserved to be destroyed because of the people's sin and declared, "Ah, Lord God! Behold, You have made the heavens and the earth by Your great power and outstretched arm. There is nothing too hard for You" (Ezekiel 3:17). God repeated Jeremiah's affirmation, saying, "Behold, I am the Lord, the God of all flesh. Is there anything too hard for Me?" (Ezekiel 3:27), and then declared that after the destruction of the city and the exile of the people, the city and the nation would be restored. And it was.

In Mark 9, a man brought his demon-possessed son to Jesus but was struggling to believe that Jesus could heal him. Jesus said, "All things are possible to him who believes" (Mark 9:23), and then healed the boy.

---

[86] May 29, 1974.

In Luke 1, the angel Gabriel came to Mary and told her that she would give birth to the Messiah. Mary wondered how that could happen since she was a virgin. But the angel affirmed that it would indeed happen and that her older, barren cousin Elizabeth would also have a child. And God declared, "With God nothing will be impossible" (Luke 1:37).

All of these passages demonstrate that God has the power to do anything, no matter how impossible the situation appears.

According[87]

Note these verses:
• "And we know that all things work together for good to those who love God, to those who are the called **according** to His purpose" (Romans 8:28).
• "And my God shall supply all your need **according** to His riches in glory by Christ Jesus" (Philippians 4:19).
• Paul prayed that the Colossian Christians would be "strengthened with all might, **according** to His glorious power" (Colossians1:11).
• "To this end I also labor, striving **according** to His working which works in me mightily" (Colossians 1:29).
Note that things are done in accordance with God's will and power.

---

[87] Written January 7, 1975, delivered to Goodwill Bible Class, September 20, 1978.

Problems[88]

We all face problems. What should we do when problems appear? Consider these statements of Jesus:

• "If you have faith as a mustard seed, you will say to this mountain, 'Move from here to there,' and it will move; and nothing will be impossible for you" (Matthew 17:20).

• "If you have faith as a mustard seed, you can say to this mulberry tree, 'Be pulled up by the roots and be planted in the sea,' and it would obey you" (Luke 17:6).

• "Whoever says to this mountain, 'Be removed and be cast into the sea,' and does not doubt in his heart, but believes that those things he says will be done, he will have whatever he says. Therefore I say to you, whatever things you ask when you pray, believe that you receive them, and you will have them (Mark 11:23-24).

These statements were made on three different occasions. Note how specific they are: *this* mountain, *this* mulberry tree, *this* mountain. When you pray asking God to remove mountains, be specific and definite. Ask God to remove your mountains (problems) one at a time.

Guidance

God repeatedly assures those who believe in Him that He will guide them:

• "I will instruct you and teach you in the way you should go; I will guide you with My eye" (Psalm 32:8).

• "The steps of a good man are ordered by the Lord, and He delights in his way" (Psalm 37:23).

• "The path of the just is like the shining sun, that shines ever brighter unto the perfect day" (Proverbs 4:18).

---

[88] May 1975.

- "I am continually with You; You hold me by my right hand" (Psalm 73:23).
- "The Lord will guide you continually" (Isaiah 58:11).
- "Teach me Your way, O Lord, and lead me in a smooth path, because of my enemies" (Psalm 27:11).
- "You are my rock and my fortress; therefore, for Your name's sake, lead me and guide me" (Psalm 31:3).
- "I will bring the blind by a way they did not know; I will lead them in paths they have not known. I will make darkness light before them, and crooked places straight" (Isaiah 42:16).
- "I form the light and create darkness, I make peace and create calamity" (Isaiah 45:7). The Living Bible more plainly states, "I send good times and bad."
- "I am the Lord your God, who teaches you to profit, who leads you by the way you should go" Isaiah 48:17).
- "Commit your way to the Lord, trust also in Him, and He shall bring it to pass." (Psalm37:5)
- "Search me, O God, and know my heart; try me, and know my anxieties; and see if there is any wicked way in me, and lead me in the way everlasting" (Psalm 139:23-24).
- "In all your ways acknowledge Him, and He shall direct your paths" (Proverbs 3:6).

The Reality of Christmas
1 John 4:9-16; Galatians 4:4-7

Do we sometimes get into a rut at Christmas? Here in our country, we have been hearing this story all our lives. At Christmas, we hear the tidings of great joy over and over until they become so familiar that they lose their meaning.

The book *The Word and the Way* tells the story of Paul Levertoff. He was a Russian Jew who studied to be a rabbi. One day in a public park, he was handed a Gospel of John. He sat down to read it and rose up a Christian believer. The book suggested that perhaps Christianity can become a substitute for a real encounter with Jesus Himself.

In Galatians, Paul was trying to show the reality and greatness of Christ.

When the Fullness of Time Had Come

In Isaiah 9:6-7, the Saviour had been promised, and then we find this being fulfilled in the New Testament:

• John the Baptist proclaimed: "The time is fulfilled, and the kingdom of God is at hand. Repent, and believe in the gospel" (Mark 1:15).

• Jesus said: "Do not think that I came to destroy the Law or the Prophets. I did not come to destroy but to fulfill" (Matthew 5:17).

These verses serve as a reminder that God always keeps His promises, beginning in Genesis and continuing to the end. When we are discouraged, we should remember that perhaps it isn't God's time yet. People in Bible times waited for the Messiah to come, but He came at God's appointed time:

• "When the fullness of the time had come, God sent forth His Son, born of a woman, born under the law to redeem those who were under the law, that we might receive the adoption as sons" (Galatians 4:4-5).

• "In this the love of God was manifested toward us, that God has sent His only begotten Son into the world, that we might live through Him" (1 John 4:9).

• "In the beginning was the Word, and the Word was with God, and the Word was God. He was in the beginning with God" (John 1:1-2).

Why did Christ come?

1. To Redeem Us

• Galatians 4:5 says that Christ came "to redeem those who were under the law." "To redeem" means "to buy back." We were bought back from the power of sin and Satan.

• "For you know the grace of our Lord Jesus Christ, that though He was rich, yet for your sakes He became poor, that you through His poverty might become rich" (2 Corinthians 8:9).

• "God was in Christ reconciling the world to Himself" (2 Corinthians 5:19). "Reconcile" means to restore friendship after a time of estrangement.

• "If anyone is in Christ, he is a new creation" (2 Corinthians 5:17).

2. To Make Us God's Children

• "God sent forth His Son, born of a woman, born under the law, to redeem those who were under the law, that we might receive the adoption as sons" (Galatians 4:4-5).

• "As many as received Him, to them He gave the right to become children of God" (John 1:12).

3. To Bring Us New Life

We cannot become sons by adoption alone because our nature is different from God's nature. Therefore, He gives us His very life by the Holy Spirit.

• "If anyone is in Christ, he is a new creation" (2 Corinthians 5:17).

• "I have been crucified with Christ; it is no longer I who live, but Christ lives in me; and the life which I now live in the flesh I live by faith in the Son of God, who loved me and gave Himself for me" (Galatians 2:20).

4. To Make Us His Heirs

• "And because you are sons, God has sent forth the Spirit of His Son into your hearts, crying out, 'Abba, Father!' Therefore you are no longer a slave but a son, and if a son, then an heir of God through Christ" (Galatians 4:6-7).

• "Eye has not seen, nor ear heard, nor have entered into the heart of man the things which God has prepared for those who love Him" (1 Corinthians 2:9).

When we get discouraged, let us remember that if we have accepted Jesus, we are children of God and that "in all these things we are more than conquerors through Him who loved us" (Romans 8:37). It is so easy to just accept "these things," the things that trouble us, but is that really conquering? "Thanks be to God who always leads us in triumph in Christ" (2Corinthians 2:14).

The Wonders of
the Christmas Story[89]

If human beings had been planning the Christmas story and arranging for the coming of Jesus, the Son of God and King of kings, how would it have been done? What preparations would we have expected to be made? Announcements in the newspapers and arrangements for TV coverage? Heads of state being invited to be there, as well as the Pope and Billy Graham? Famous choirs and orchestras asked to perform?

God's preparations for this great event had more of a personal nature. Announcements had been made, through Moses (Deuteronomy 18:18) and the prophets (e.g., Isaiah 7:14). The angel of the Lord visited Zechariah (Luke 1:5-20), Mary (Luke 1:26-38), and Joseph in a dream (Matthew 1:18-25). The wise men came to Bethlehem because of a special star (Matthew 2:1-2). God also spoke to the wise men (Matthew 2:12) and to Joseph in another dream (Matthew 2:13).

An article called "The Impossibles of Christmas" stated that "When God is about to do something great, He starts with a difficulty. When He is about to do something magnificent, He starts with an impossibility." When the angel Gabriel appeared to Mary, he told her: "With God nothing will be impossible" (Luke 1:37). Do we think it was just a coincidence that "a decree went out from Caesar Augustus that all the world should be registered...So all went to be registered, everyone to his own city" (Luke 2:1-3)? Did it just happen that a star led the wise men to Bethlehem? Or that an angel appeared to Zechariah, Mary, and Joseph—and also the shepherds (Luke 2:8-14)? That is not how we would have done it, but is it not more wonderful and surprising? Have we become so familiar with the Christmas story that it loses its wonder?

---

[89] Goodwill Bible Class, December 5, 1984.

It is sobering to recognize that some people missed out on participating in the greatest miracle in history. The religious leaders of the day missed out because they were expecting the Messiah to come in a different way.

Are we in danger of missing some of the wonders of Christmas? There are so many nice things about Christmas—meeting and entertaining friends, reading Christmas mail, visiting Christmas panoramas, enjoying TV specials (some are silly but there are some good ones too, celebrating unselfishness). There is time for everything we really want to do. Don't let the things that matter be crowded out by the things that don't matter much.

Can This Be Christmas?

What's all this hectic rush and worry?
Where go these crowds who run and curry?
Why all the lights—the Christmas trees?
The jolly "fat man," tell me please!
Why, don't you know? This is the day
For parties and for fun and play;
Why this is Christmas!
So this is Christmas, do you say?
But where is Christ this Christmas day?
Has He been lost among the throng?
His voice drowned out by empty song?
No. He's not here—you'll find Him where
Some humble soul now kneels in prayer,
Who knows the Christ of Christmas.
But see the many aimless thousands
Who gather on this Christmas Day,
Whose hearts have never yet been opened,
Or said to Him, "Come in to stay."
In countless homes the candles burning,
In countless hearts expectant yearning
For gifts and presents, food and fun,
And laughter till the day is done.
But not a tear of grief or sorrow

For Him so poor He had to borrow
A crib, a colt, a boat, a bed
Where He could lay His weary head.
I'm tired of all this empty celebration,
Of feasting, drinking, recreation;
I'll go instead to Calvary.
And there I'll kneel with those who know
The meaning of that manger low,
And find the Christ—this Christmas.
I leap by faith across the years
To that great day when He appears
The second time, to rule and reign,
To end all sorrow, death, and pain.
In endless bliss we then shall dwell
With Him who saved our souls from hell,
And worship Christ—not Christmas![90]

Christmas Gifts

Recently, I was given an azalea plant. It was big, Christmasy, and lovely. But where was I going to put it? In the end, I sent some of my other plants down to the basement for a few weeks to make room for it.

God has offered us some wonderful gifts too. Do we hesitate to accept them because we like things as they are and don't want to bother changing things around? Here are some of the gifts God offers us:

Peace: "Peace I leave with you, My peace I give to you; not as the world gives do I give to you. Let not your heart be troubled, neither let it be afraid" (John 14:27). "Be anxious for nothing, but in everything by prayer and supplication, with thanksgiving, let your requests be made known to God; and the peace of God, which surpasses all understanding, will guard

---

[90] M.R. DeHaan (1891-1965), Founder, Radio Bible Class.

your hearts and minds through Christ Jesus" (Philippians 4:6-7).

Eternal Life. "The gift of God is eternal life in Christ Jesus our Lord" (Romans 6:23). When we are saved by God, we are freed from our sins and become servants of God: "You are not your own...you were bought at a price" (1 Corinthains 6:19-20).

Strength. "Those who wait on the Lord shall renew their strength; they shall mount up with wings like eagles, they shall run and not be weary, they shall walk and not faint" (Isaiah 40:31).

Material Needs. "My God shall supply all your need according to His riches in glory by Christ Jesus" Philippians 4:19). "Seek the kingdom of God, and all these things shall be added to you" (Luke 12:30).

Love. The group[91] last Sunday night said that our greatest need is to know that someone loves us. Paul said, "I live by faith in the Son of God, who loved me and gave Himself for me" (Galatians 2:20). God promised: "I have loved you with an everlasting love" (Jeremiah 31:3). Remember that "the things which are seen are temporary, but the things which are not seen are eternal" (2 Corinthians 4:18).

Christmas Gifts 2[92]

As the Christmas season approaches, Christmas shopping occupies much of our time. We write out a list and start making gifts, or we hurry from store to store purchasing presents for loved ones or for those who will give to us. When Christmas Day comes, there is all the excitement of unwrapping our parcels. As we open the gifts, let us not forget that Christmas is the anniversary of the greatest gift ever given: "For God so loved the world that He gave His only begotten Son, that

---

[91] The group was called ACOA, possibly Adult Children of Alcoholics?
[92] Ladies Aid, December 11, 1958.

whoever believes in Him should not perish but have everlasting life" (John 3:16).

But John also tells us: "He was in the world, and the world was made through Him, and the world did not know Him. He came to His own, and His own did not receive Him" (John 1:10-11). Do we today neglect this greatest gift of God? If we gave someone a present and they didn't even bother to open it, wouldn't we think them ungrateful? Millions in the world today have never heard the gospel message and had the opportunity of believing in Jesus, but many who have heard are refusing to accept it.

Perhaps we do believe that Jesus is our Saviour and Lord but haven't bothered to think about God's other gifts to us. It is almost as though someone wired our house for electricity and gave us all kinds of appliances to use with it. But perhaps we just turn on the electric lights and get along without the vacuum cleaner, washing machine, and other appliances that would make life easier for us. The Christian life should be one of continual growth, and the farther we go, the more we should realize God's greatness and His goodness to us. What are some of these gifts that God has promised us?

1. Peace. The angels sang of peace on earth. Jesus said, "Peace I leave with you, My peace I give to you" (John 14:27).

2. Rest. "Come to Me, all you who labor and are heavy laden, and I will give you rest. Take My yoke upon you and learn from Me, for I am gentle and lowly in heart, and you will find rest for your souls" (Matthew 11:28-29).

3. Strength. "Those who wait on the Lord shall renew their strength" (Isaiah 40:31). "My grace is sufficient for you, for My strength is made perfect in weakness" (2 Corinthians 12:9).

4. Material Needs. "My God shall supply all your need according to His riches in glory by Christ Jesus" (Philippians 4:19). Jesus told His disciples: "Your Father knows that you need these things. But seek the kingdom of God, and all these things shall be added to you" (Luke 12:30-31).

5. Eternal Life. "The wages of sin is death, but the gift of God is eternal life in Christ Jesus our Lord" (Romans 6:23). "By grace you have been saved through faith, and that not of yourselves; it is the gift of God" (Ephesians 2:8).

The Bible is filled with passages on the riches of God and with verses on His promises, which are available to us if we only ask for them and fulfill the conditions. God "is able to do exceedingly abundantly above all that we ask or think" (Ephesians 3:20). I looked in the Concordance for verses on gifts and was amazed at the number and variety of them. The more we study them, the more we realize God's greatness and become like David, who said, "When I consider Your heavens, the work of Your fingers, the moon and the stars, which You have ordained, what is man that You are mindful of him, and the son of man that You visit him? For You have made him a little lower than the angels, and You have crowned him with glory and honor" (Psalm 8:3-5). Do we at Christmas give God praise, or do we sing Christmas carols without reflecting on their meaning?

In return for all of God's goodness to us, what can we give Him? Perhaps the greatest gift we can give is the gift of ourselves. As we give Him this gift, may we also dedicate to Him our time, our talents, and our possessions. In 1 Corinthians 12, Paul speaks of the spiritual gifts that each person has been given. Although all are members of one body, each has a different talent. Some are given the gift of teaching, some the gift of healing, some are apostles, and some are prophets. Each of us has been given a gift that we can use for God. Timothy was reminded by Paul to "stir up the gift of God which is in you" (2 Timothy 1:6). Perhaps some of our gifts need stirring up too. Let us at Christmas put some of our talents to use for Him, for the only worthwhile gifts come from the heart.

Power, Apollo 8, and an Ice Storm[93]

This Christmas season in some ways has been an unusual one. Have you noticed what seems to be the chief topic of conversation when people get together? During Christmas week, besides the celebration of Christmas, most people were discussing the flight of Apollo 8 around the moon and what the men's chances were of making a safe return. It was thrilling to hear the reading of Genesis 1 from the moon. We were impressed by the tremendous amount of power required for their journey and the fact that God's laws were so dependable that they were able to time their return to almost the exact second and place.

Then, the day after the astronauts landed, there was the ice storm in Waterford, and we, too, returned to earth with a jolt and concentrated on keeping warm and fed. Since then, the topic of conversation has been: How did you manage during the storm? This time, it was not power that impressed us but the lack of it.

For that reason, I have chosen a few verses on power. God's Word is a powerhouse from beginning to end:
• "In the beginning God created the heavens and the earth" (Genesis 1:1).
• "Have you not known? Have you not heard? The everlasting God, the Lord, the Creator of the ends of the earth, neither faints nor is weary. His understanding is unsearchable. He gives power to the weak, and to those who have no might He increases strength. Even the youths shall faint and be weary, and the young men shall utterly fall, but those who wait on the Lord shall renew their strength; they shall mount up with wings like eagles, they shall run and not be weary, they shall walk and not faint" (Isaiah 40:28-31).

---

[93] Mission Circle, January 1970.

• "Most assuredly, I say to you, he who believes in Me, the works that I do he will do also; and greater works than these he will do, because I go to My Father. And whatever you ask in My name, that I will do, that the Father may be glorified in the Son. If you ask anything in My name, I will do it" (John 14:12-14).

• "'But you shall receive power when the Holy Spirit has come upon you; and you shall be witnesses to Me in Jerusalem, and in all Judea and Samaria, and to the end of the earth.' Now when [Jesus] had spoken these things, while they watched, He was taken up, and a cloud received Him out of their sight" (Acts 1:8-9).

• "For God has not given us a spirit of fear, but of power and of love and of a sound mind" (2 Timothy 1:7).

• "But as many as received him, to them gave he power to become the sons of God, even to them that believe on his name" (John 1:12, KJV).

On the last night of the ice storm, like most people, we went to bed by lamplight. About 3:00 a.m., we awakened, and there seemed to be a green light coming through the window. When we looked out, everything was in darkness except for several fires burning along the side of the street. The hydro line had broken and was burning steadily. It was a rather frightening experience. After I got back to bed, I couldn't help but think of all that power going to waste when so many people needed it.

Perhaps there is a spiritual application. God is a source of power. We read these promises in the Bible and wonder why our lives are not more powerful. The Bible is full of stories of what people have been able to accomplish by God's Spirit working through them. We don't have to know everything about electricity in order to use it, and the same is true with God's power. As we start this new year, wouldn't it be a good idea if we investigated more of how this power works?

We are told in Matthew 24:12 that because iniquity will abound, the love of many will grow cold. Sometimes our lives become cold and ice-covered, and through neglect sometimes there is a break in our power connection with God. Sometimes there is a serious break and all we can do is be patient and await the repair crew. Have you ever noticed the number of verses in the Bible about waiting?

At other times, all we need to do is turn on the switch. The night of the storm, we were in darkness, and then we looked out and saw bright lights in our neighbour's house. After groping our way to the switch, we found that we, too, had light. Perhaps prayer might be likened to the switch that connects us to God.

Sometimes the trouble with the power lines abates when the sun comes out and melts the ice. So, too, God's love to us is powerful and able to melt the ice of indifference. God's love working through us is also powerful enough to break through barriers.

With hydro, there is a monthly bill. Sometimes there is a price to be paid in the Christian life, but it is worth it. It seems to me that this involves a surrender of our will to God and a willingness to be used by Him.

As we further investigate the power of God, we probably won't take a trip around the moon, but we are told: "For the Lord Himself will descend from heaven with a shout, with the voice of an archangel, and with the trumpet of God. And the dead in Christ will rise first. Then we who are alive and remain shall be caught up together with them in the clouds to meet the Lord in the air. And thus we shall always be with the Lord" (1 Thessalonians 4:16-17). That is great power. When we hear a noise in the sky, it is a reminder that we have the privilege of putting God to work. There is a sense in which God has limited Himself and works for human beings only at their request. If we ask, He can clean up our past, help us to realize our dreams, and guide us in the future.

Steps⁹⁴

I have been thinking lately about my life's journey. Proverbs 4:12 says, "When you walk, your steps will not be hindered, and when you run, you will not stumble." The Hebrew has the sense of "As you go step by step, the way shall open up before you." There are many other Bible verses that talk about our life as a journey:

• "The path of the just is like the shining sun, that shines ever brighter unto the perfect day" (Proverbs 4:18).

• "He knows the way that I take; when He has tested me, I shall come forth as gold" (Job 23:10).

• "The steps of a good man are ordered by the Lord, and He delights in his way...The law of his God is in his heart; none of his steps shall slide" (Psalm 137:23,31)

• "A man's heart plans his way, but the Lord directs his steps" (Proverbs 16:9).

• "O Lord, I know the way of man is not in himself; it is not in man who walks to direct his own steps" (Jeremiah 10:23).

• "To this you were called, because Christ also suffered for us, leaving us an example, that you should follow His steps" (1 Peter 2:21).

• "Does He not see my ways, and count all my steps?" (Job 31:4).

• "You enlarged my path under me, so my feet did not slip" (Psalm 18:36).

• "You will show me the path of life; in Your presence is fullness of joy; at Your right hand are pleasures forevermore" (Psalm 16:11).

• "Show me Your ways, O Lord; teach me Your paths" (Psalm 25:4).

• "He leads me in the paths of righteousness for His name's sake" (Psalm 23:3).

---

⁹⁴ May 11, 1999.

• "Happy is the man who finds wisdom...Her ways are ways of pleasantness, and all her paths are peace" (Proverbs 3:13,17).

Prayer[95]

Our Heavenly Father,

We thank You for this opportunity of joining together in worship. We thank You for Your goodness to us, not only in providing us with the things we need but also in surrounding us with the beauty of autumn.

As we think of Your greatness and holiness, we are reminded of our sins, which separate us from You. We ask forgiveness for the things we have said or done that have hurt others, for the tasks which we have neglected or postponed till a more convenient time. We ask forgiveness for putting ourselves first, for thinking too much of what we want and forgetting the needs of others. Help us to realize that none of us can get through life on our own but we are dependent on You for life itself.

We pray for those who have problems and worries this morning, and we ask that You will show them the answers. We try to avoid trials and suffering, but we also realize that often through them we are drawn closer to You and learn just how much You love and care for each one of us—a love so great that Jesus died for our sins on the cross.

We pray this morning for those who are ill and those who are in hospital, that You will meet their needs, and we pray, too, for their families and those who care for them.

We thank You for Your protection and guidance during the past week and for the way in which You have answered our prayers. We pray for those who are indifferent and for those who are too busy to take time to worship, that they may realize how much they are missing.

---

[95] Prayer at the Thanksgiving Service in 1981.

We pray for the needs of our local church and Sunday school. We ask that You will give strength and wisdom to those in positions of leadership. We pray for our pastor on vacation, that he may return feeling renewed in body and spirit.

We thank You for this country of Canada and for the many blessings we enjoy. Please give wisdom and guidance to those in authority over us, that they may make the right decisions.

We pray, too, for the work of the Baptist Women's Missionary Society and the Overseas Missions Board. We pray for all the missionaries who serve in India and Bolivia, in Kenya and Brazil, and in many other countries, and also for those here in Canada. We ask that You will bless our speaker, Miss Ricketts, and give her the message we need to hear. We ask that You will give her strength and help for the work she is doing among the international students in Toronto.

We thank You for Your love for each one of us and ask that each person here may realize Your presence and that You will guide and direct us during the coming week.

May everything in this service be according to Your will and honouring to You. We pray in the name of Jesus Christ our Lord. Amen.

Benediction

May the grace of the Lord Jesus Christ and the love of God and the communion of the Holy Spirit be with you all. Amen.

Prayer 2 [96]

Our Heavenly Father,

We thank You for the lovely day that You have given us. We thank You for Your care and protection during the past week and for the many ways in which You have met our needs.

---

[96] September 26, 1999. Waterford Baptist Church had been a solid church for many years. At this point, it was beginning to lose its focus and was entering a period of decline.

May each one present here be conscious of Your great love for him or her—a love so great that Jesus came down to earth and died on the cross for our sins and rose again from the dead so that if we believe on Him we may have everlasting life.

We praise You for Your holiness and for Your mighty power which created this world.

We are conscious of the sin which separates us from You. We ask forgiveness for the wrong things we have said or done and for the things we have left undone. We ask You to forgive us for the times we have put ourselves first. Help us to realize that we are dependent on You for life itself and it could be cut off at any time.

We thank you for our country of Canada and the freedom we enjoy. We ask that You will give guidance and wisdom to those in government over us and that they may recognize You as the Supreme Ruler.

We thank You for this church and its leaders over the years. We pray for our pastor, deacons, trustees, and those in leadership positions that they may ask Your will and that we may all work together in harmony.

We pray this morning for the people of Taiwan and Turkey, who are suffering because of earthquakes, and those on the Atlantic coast, which has been hit with hurricanes. We pray for those in East Timor and other countries, where there is civil war. As Your Word goes out today, may they come to learn of You.

We do not understand why so many of our congregation have been overcome by illness, but You know each one by name, and we ask You to help. We pray for all those who have family or financial problems, that You will meet their need as they turn to You. We ask Your comfort for those who are bereaved.

We do not ask for less stressful lives, for we realize that it is the only way for us to become strong by depending on Your mighty power. We pray that You will give us strength for each day as it comes.

We pray for the leaders of Baptist Missions and for those engaged in the work of the Baptist Women's Missionary Society. We thank You for Pat Fisher and the work she is doing in Brantford. We pray that it may be a means of many coming to know Christ.

May each person here have a new understanding of the things You are trying to teach us, and may we be strengthened for the tasks of the coming week.

May everything in this service be according to Your will and honouring to You.

We ask these things in the name of Jesus Christ our Lord. Amen.